March of America Facsimile Series
Number 43

Travels and Adventures in Canada

Alexander Henry

Travels and Adventures
in Canada
by *Alexander Henry*

ANN ARBOR

UNIVERSITY MICROFILMS, INC.

A Subsidiary of Xerox Corporation

56765

Foreword

Victories over the French at Quebec in 1759 and at Montreal in 1760 gave the English a *de facto* possession of Canada which was later confirmed by the Treaty of Paris in 1763. It took some time, though, for the change of sovereignty to be accepted by the Indians and by the French Canadians living in the frontier regions. The initial resistance encountered by the British government in the interior of Canada and the gradual establishment of order there is well described by Alexander Henry, one of the first traders to enter Canada following the British conquest. His reminiscences, published in 1809 under the title *Travels And Adventures in Canada and The Indian Territories,* cover the critical first years of English rule from 1760 to 1776. Henry's involvement in the fur trade allowed him to furnish much information about that subject too. But probably it is the wealth of detail he provides about the Indians in the Great Lakes region and on the plains that will be adjudged his greatest contribution.

Henry, originally from New Jersey, had barely turned twenty when he accompanied the expedition of General Amherst against Montreal in 1760. The following year Henry determined to go to Michilimackinac—a region, he had been told, that was richer in furs than any other part of the world. Upon his arrival he began to hear rumblings of Indian discontent, the prelude to Pontiac's Conspiracy. One of the Indian chiefs summed up their sentiments when he said to Henry, "Englishman, although you have conquered the French, you have not conquered us!"

In June, 1763, the Indians surprised the garrison at Fort Michilimackinac and massacred almost all of the English. The author, unobserved during the attack, looked on in horror. "The dead were scalped and mangled; the dying were writhing and shrieking, under the unsatiated knife and tomahawk." Henry managed to conceal himself for a while but eventually his hiding place was discovered. Fortunately for him, he was taken prisoner rather than killed on the spot. During the next year he lived with the Indians, fearful that each day might be his last.

Finally the Indians released him in June, 1764, at Fort Niagara. Thereupon General Bradstreet induced him to join an expedition for the relief of Detroit. The author terminates the first part of his account at the peace which ensued shortly thereafter.

The second part of the book is concerned with the period which succeeded the Pontiac Conspiracy. Having received an exclusive right of trade in the Lake Superior area, Henry began to exploit his advantage. For a time he also became interested in a mining company, but the venture proved a failure and the company was dissolved. The high point of these years was undoubtedly Henry's trip to the plains. He had departed from Beaver Lake in January, 1776, with the intention of going all the way to the Rocky Mountains. Although the Indians later dissuaded him from his goal, he nevertheless penetrated deep into the plains region and had an opportunity to observe closely the customs of the Indians living there. His narrative closes with his return to Montreal in October, 1776, where he learned of the repulse of the invasion of Canada by the rebellious colonists to the south.

Henry's account was obviously written some time after the events he describes. It therefore contains errors of fact which might be expected from occasional lapses of memory. But in essential matters, Henry is considered a reliable witness. More background about the author and his book can be found in the introduction written by Milo M. Quaife to *Alexander Henry's Travels and Adventures* (Chiago, 1921), pp. xiii-xxiv. See also Raymond McCoy, *The Massacre of Old Fort Mackinac* (Bay City, 1946).

Engraved by P. Maverick from an Original Miniature.

ALEXANDER HENRY.

New York Published by I. Riley. 1809.

TRAVELS

AND ADVENTURES

IN

CANADA

AND

THE INDIAN TERRITORIES,

BETWEEN

THE YEARS 1760 AND 1776.

IN TWO PARTS.

BY ALEXANDER HENRY, ESQ.

NEW-YORK:

PRINTED AND PUBLISHED BY I. RILEY.

••••

1809.

TO

THE RIGHT HONOURABLE

SIR JOSEPH BANKS, BARONET ;

KNIGHT-COMPANION

OF THE MOST HONOURABLE ORDER OF THE BATH ;

ONE OF HIS MAJESTY'S

MOST HONOURABLE PRIVY COUNCIL;

PRESIDENT OF THE ROYAL SOCIETY, F. S. A.

&c. &c. &c.

THIS VOLUME

WITH GREAT DEFERENCE,

IS MOST RESPECTFULLY , DEDICATED,

BY

HIS VERY DEVOTED,

AND VERY HUMBLE SERVANT,

ALEXANDER HENRY.

Montreal, October 20th, 1809.

John Henry Esq[r]

Montreal 14 September 1819

Dear Sir

It is a long time since we
had the pleasure of hearing from you, we expected
you and your lady would have favourd us with
a visit this summer, we were all much troubled
when we heard of the steam boat of Lake Champlain
being burst, a friend of yours being on board with

Daughter Eliza. Mrs Buthurst, is very unwell, but hope nothing dangerous, I enclose in this the Bills for _____ dollars, with which you will purchase for me one Lottery Ticket, and please send me the number. Mrs Henry & _____ join in our best wishes for you Mrs Henry & all the family and remain your old friend & humble Serv ——

Alexander Henry ——

PREFACE.

A PREMATURE attempt to share in the fur-trade of Canada, directly on the conquest of the country, led the author of the following pages into situations of some danger and singularity ; and the pursuit, under better auspices, of the same branch of commerce, occasioned him to visit various parts of the Indian Territories.

These transactions occupied a period of sixteen years, commencing nearly with the author's setting out in life. The details, from time to time committed to paper, form the subject matter of the present volume.

The heads, under which, for the most part, they will be found to range themselves are three: first, the incidents or adventures in which the author was engaged; secondly, the observations, on the geography and natural history of the countries visited, which he was able to make, and to preserve;

and, thirdly, the views of society and manners, among a part of the Indians of North America, which it has belonged to the course of his narrative to develope.

Upon the last, the author may be permitted to remark, that he has by no means undertaken to write the general history of the American Indians, nor any theory of their morals, or their merits. With but few exceptions, it has been the entire scope of his design, simply to relate those particular facts, which are either identified with his own fortunes, or with the truth of which he is otherwise personally conversant. All comment, therefore, in almost all instances, is studiously avoided.

MONTREAL, October 20th, 1809.

PART THE FIRST.

TRAVELS

AND ADVENTURES,

&c. &c.

———

CHAPTER I.

Journies and Voyages between Oswegatchie and Montréal. Indian encampments. Indian hospitality. Winter travelling, in the wilder parts of Canada. Les Cédres, the uppermost white settlement on the river Saint-Lawrence. Author prepares for a voyage to Michilimackinac.

IN the year 1760, when the British arms, under General Amherst, were employed in the reduction of Canada, I accompanied the expedition, which, subsequently to the surrender of Quebec,* descended from Oswego, on Lake Ontario, against Fort de Levi, one of the upper posts, situate on an island, which lies on the south side of the great river, Saint-Lawrence, at a short distance below the mouth of

* Quebec surrendered on the 18th of September, 1759.

the Oswegatchie. Fort de Levi surrendered on the 21st day of August, seven days after the commencement of the siege; and General Amherst continued his voyage down the stream, carrying his forces against Montréal.

It happened, that in this voyage, one of the few fatal accidents, which are remembered to have occurred, in that dangerous part of the river, below Lake Saint-Français, called the Rapides des Cédres, befel the British army. Several boats, loaded with provisions and military stores, were lost, together with upward of a hundred men. I had three boats, loaded with merchandize, all of which were lost; and I saved my life, only by gaining the bottom of one of my boats, which lay among the rocky shelves, and on which I continued for some hours, and until I was kindly taken off, by one of the general's aides-de-camp.

The surrender of Montréal, and, with it, the surrender of all Canada, followed that of Fort de Levi, at only the short interval of three days; and, proposing to avail myself of the new market, which was thus thrown open to British adventure, I hastened to Albany, where my commercial connections were, and where I procured a quantity of goods, with which I sat out, intending to carry them to Montréal. For this, however, the winter was too near approached; I was able only to return to Fort de Levi, to which the conquerors had now given the name of Fort William-Augustus, and where I remained until the month of January, in the following year.

At this time, having disposed of my goods to the garrison, and the season, for travelling on the snow and ice, being set in, I prepared to go down to Montréal. The journey was to be performed through a country, inhabited only by Indians and by beasts of the forest, and which presented to the eye no other change, than from thick woods, to the broad surface of a frozen river. It was necessary that I should be accompanied, as well by an interpreter as by a guide, to both of which ends, I engaged the services of a Canadian, named John-Baptist Bodoine.

The snow, which lay upon the ground, was, by this time, three feet in depth. The hour of departure arriving, I left the fort, on snow-shoes, an article of equipment which I had never used before, and which I found it not a little difficult to manage. I did not avoid frequent falls; and, when down, I was scarcely able to rise.

At sunset, on the first day, we reached an Indian encampment, of six lodges and about twenty men. As these people had been very recently employed offensively, against the English, in the French service, I agreed but reluctantly to the proposal, of my guide and interpreter, which was nothing less, than that we should pass the night with them. My fears were somewhat lulled by his information, that he was personally acquainted with those who composed the camp, and by his assurances, that no danger was to be apprehended ; and, being greatly fatigued, I entered one of the lodges, where I presently fell asleep.

Unfortunately, Bodoine had brought, upon his back, a small keg of rum, which, while I slept, he opened, not only for himself, but for the general gratification of his friends; a circumstance, of which I was first made aware, in being awakened, by a kick on the breast, from the foot of one of my hosts, and by a yell, or Indian cry, which immediately succeeded. At the instant of opening my eyes, I saw that my assailant was struggling with one of his companions, who, in conjunction with several women, was endeavouring to restrain his ferocity. Perceiving, however, in the countenance of my enemy, the most determined mischief, I sprung upon my feet, receiving, in so doing, a wound in my hand, from a knife, which had been raised to give a more serious wound. While the rest of my guardians continued their charitable efforts for my protection, an old woman took hold of my arm, and, making signs that I should accompany her, led me out of the lodge, and then gave me to understand, that unless I fled, or could conceal myself, I should certainly be killed.

My guide was absent; and, without his direction, I was at a loss where to go. In all the surrounding lodges, there was the same howling and violence, as in that from which I had escaped. I was without my snow-shoes, and had only so much clothing as I had fortunately left upon me, when I lay down to sleep. It was now one o'clock in the morning, in the month of January, and in a a climate of extreme rigour.

I was unable to address a single word, in her own language, to the old woman who had thus befriended me ; but, on repeating the name of Bodoine, I soon found that she' comprehended my meaning; and, having first pointed to a large tree, behind which, she made signs, that until she could find my guide, I should hide myself, she left me, on this important errand. Meanwhile, I made my way to the tree, and seated myself in the snow. From my retreat, I beheld several Indians, running from one lodge to another, as if to quell the disturbance which prevailed.

The coldness of the atmosphere congealed the blood about my wound, and prevented further bleeding ; and the anxious state of my mind rendered me almost insensible to bodily suffering. At the end of half an hour, I heard myself called, by Bodoine, whom, on going to him, I found as much intoxicated, and as much a savage, as the Indians themselves ; but, he was nevertheless able to fetch my snow-shoes, from the lodge in which I had left them, and to point out to me a beaten path, which presently entered a deep wood, and which he told me I must follow.

After walking about three miles, I heard, at length, the foot-steps of my guide, who had now overtaken me. I thought it most prudent to abstain from all reproof ; and we proceeded on our march till sun-rise, when we arrived at a solitary Indian hunting-lodge, built with branches of trees, and of which the only inhabitants were an Indian and his wife. Here, the warmth of a large fire reconciled me to a second experiment on Indian hospitality. The result was very different from that of the one which had preceded it ; for, after relieving my thirst with melted snow, and my hunger with a plentiful meal of venison, of which there was a great quantity in the lodge, and which was liberally set before me, I resumed my journey, full of sentiments of gratitude, such as almost obliterated the recollection of what had befallen me, among the friends of my benefactors.

From the hunting-lodge, I followed my guide till evening, when we encamped on the banks of the Saint-Lawrence, making a fire, and sup-

ping on the meat with which our wallets had been
filled in the morning.

While I indulged myself in rest, my guide visited the shore, where he discovered a bark canoe,
which had been left there, in the beginning of the
winter, by some Indian way-farers. We were now
at the head of the Longue Sault, one of those por-
tions of the river, in which it passes over a shallow,
inclining and rocky bed, and where its motion consequently prevents it from freezing, even in the cold-
est part of the year ; and my guide, as soon as he
had made his discovery, recommended, that we
should go by water down the *rapids*, as the means
of saving time, of shortening our journey, and of
avoiding a numerous body of Indians, then hunting on the banks below. The last of these arguments was, with me, so powerful, that though a
bark canoe was a vehicle to which I was altogether
a stranger ; though this was a very small one,
of only sixteen or eighteen feet in length,* and
much out of repair; and though the misfortune
which I had experienced, in the navigation of these
rocky parts of the Saint-Lawrence, when descending with the army, naturally presented itself to my
mind, as a still further discouragement, yet I was
not long in resolving to undertake the voyage.

Accordingly, after stopping the leaks, as completely as we were able, we embarked, and pro-

* There are still smaller.

ceeded. My fears were not lessened, by perceiving that the least unskilful motion was sufficient to
overset the ticklish craft into which I had ventured;
by the reflection, that a shock, comparatively gentle, from a mass of rock or ice, was more than its
frail material could sustain ; nor by observing that
the ice, which lined the shores of the river, was
too strong to be pushed through, and, at the same
time, too weak to be walked upon, so that, in the
event of disaster, it would be almost impossible to reach the land.   In fact, we had not proceeded more than a mile, when our canoe became
full of water, and it was not till after a long search,
that we found a place of safety.

Treading, once more, upon dry ground, I should
willingly have faced the wilderness and all its Indians, rather than embark again; but my guide informed me that I was upon an island, and I had
therefore no choice before me. We stopped the
leaks a second time, and recommenced our voyage,
which we performed with success, but sitting, all
the way, in six inches of water.   In this manner,
we arrived at the foot of the rapids, where the
river was frozen all across.   Here, we disembarked upon the ice, walked to the bank, made a fire,
and *encamped ;* for such is the phrase employed,
in the woods of Canada.

At day-break the next morning, we put on our
snow-shoes, and commenced our journey over
the ice ; and, at ten o'clock, arrived in sight of

Lake Saint-Français, which is from four to six miles in breadth. The wind was high, and the snow, drifting over the expanse, prevented us, at times, from discovering the land, and consequently (for compass we had none) from pursuing, with certainty, our course.

Toward noon, the storm became so violent, that we directed our steps to the shore, on the north side, by the shortest route we could ; and, making a fire, dined on the remains of the Indian hunter's bounty. At two o'clock, in the afternoon, when the wind had subsided, and the atmosphere grown more clear, I discerned a *cariole*, or sledge, moving our way, and immediately sent my guide to the driver, with a request, that he would come to my encampment. On his arrival, I agreed with him to carry me to Les Cédres, a distance of eight leagues, for a reward of eight dollars. The driver was a Canadian, who had been to the Indian village of Saint-Regis, and was now on his return to Les Cédres, then the uppermost white settlement on the Saint-Lawrence.

Late in the evening, I reached Les Cédres, and was carried to the house of M. Leduc, its seignior, by whom I was politely and hospitably received. M. Leduc being disposed to converse with me, it became a subject of regret, that neither party understood the language of the other ; but, an inter-

preter was fortunately found, in the person of a
serjeant of His Majesty's Eighteenth Regiment of
Foot.

I now learned, that M. Leduc, in the earlier part
of his life, had been engaged in the fur-trade, with
the Indians of Michilimackinac and Lake Superior.
He informed me of his acquaintance with the Indian languages, and his knowledge of furs ; and
gave me to understand, that Michilimackinac was
richer, in this commodity, than any other part of
the world.   He added, that the Indians were a
peaceable race of men, and that an European might
travel, from one side of the continent to the other,
without experiencing insult.   Further, he mentioned, that a *guide*, who lived at no great distance
from his house, could confirm the truth of all that
he had advanced.

I, who had previously thought of visiting Michilimackinac, with a view to the Indian trade, gave
the strictest attention to all that fell, on this subject, from my host ; and, in order to possess myself, as far as possible, of all that might be collected
in addition, I requested, that the *guide* should be
sent for.   This man arrived ; and a short conversation terminated in my engaging him to conduct
myself, and the canoes which I was to procure,

to Michilimackinac, in the month of June following.

There being, at this time, no goods in Montréal,
adapted to the Indian trade, my next business was
to proceed to Albany, to make my purchases
there. This I did in the beginning of the month
of May, by the way of Lake Champlain ; and,
on the 15th of June, arrived again in Montréal,
bringing with me my outfits. As I was altogether a stranger to the commerce in which I was
engaging, I confided in the recommendations, giv-
en me, of one Etienne Campion, as my assistant ;
a part which he uniformly fulfilled with honesty
and fidelity.

His Excellency, General Gage, who now commanded in chief, in Canada, very reluctantly granted me the permission, at this time requisite, for
going to Michilimackinac. No treaty of peace had yet
been made, between the English and the Indians,
which latter were in arms, under Pontiac, an Indian leader, of more than common celebrity, and
General Gage was therefore strongly, and (as it
became manifest) but too justly apprehensive, that
both the property and lives of His Majesty's subjects would be very insecure, in the Indian countries. But, he had already granted such permission to a Mr. Bostwick ; and this I was able to em-

ploy, as an argument against his refusal, in respect to myself. General Gage complied ; and on the 3d day of August, 1761, after some further delay, in obtaining a passport from the town-major, I dispatched my canoes to Lachine, there to take in their lading.

CHAPTER II.

Voyage from Montréal to Michilimackinac. Ca-
noes. Canoe-men. Lachine. Saint-Anne. Lake
Des Deux Montagnes. Indian mission. Descrip-
tion of part of the river Des Outaouais. Indians,
returning from the chace—their opinion of the
Author's undertaking. Claims of the Algonquins,
on the banks of the Outaouais—their regard to
the right of property. Leave the Outaouais, and
enter the Matawa.

THE inland navigation, from Montréal to Michilimackinac, may be performed, either by the way
of Lakes, Ontario and Erie, or by the river Des
Outaouais, Lake Nipisingue and the river Des
Français ; for, as well by one as the other of these
routes, we are carried to Lake Huron. The
second is the shortest, and that which is usually
pursued by the canoes, employed in the Indian
trade.

The canoes, which I provided for my undertaking, were, as is usual, five fathom and a half
in length, and four feet and a half in their extreme breadth, and formed of birch-tree bark, a

quarter of an inch in thickness.   The bark is
lined with small splints of cedar-wood ; and the
vessel is further strengthened with ribs of the same
wood, of which the two ends are fastened to the
gunwales : several bars, rather than seats, are also
laid across the canoe, from gunwale to gunwale.
The small roots of the spruce-tree afford the
wattap, with which the bark is sewed ; and the
gum of the pine-tree supplies the place of tar
and oakum.   Bark, some spare wattap and gum,
are always carried in each canoe, for the repairs
which frequently become necessary.

The canoes are worked, not with oars, but with
paddles ; and, occasionally, with a sail.   To each
canoe there are eight men ; and to every three or
four canoes, which constitute a *brigade*, there is a
guide, or conductor.   Skilful men, at double the
wages of the rest, are placed in the head and stern.
They engage to go from Montréal to Michilimackinac, and back to Montréal again ; the mid-
dle-men at one hundred and fifty livres, and the
end-men at three hundred livres, each.*   The
guide has the command of his brigade, and is answerable for all pillage and loss ; and, in return,
every man's wages is answerable to him.   This
regulation was established under the French government.

* These particulars may be compared with those, of a
more modern date, given in the Voyages of Sir Alexander Mackenzie.

The freight of a canoe, of the substance and dimensions which I have detailed, consists in sixty *pieces*, or packages, of merchandize, of the weight of from ninety to a hundred pounds each; and provisions to the amount of one thousand weight. To this is to be added, the weight of eight men, and of eight bags, weighing forty pounds each, one of which every man is privileged to put on board. The whole weight must therefore exceed eight thousand pounds; or may perhaps be averaged at four tons.

The nature of the navigation, which is to be described, will sufficiently explain, why the canoe is the only vessel which can be employed along its course. The necessity, indeed, becomes apparent, at the very instant of our departure from Montréal itself.

The Saint-Lawrence, for several miles, immediately above Montréal, descends, with a rapid current, over a shallow rocky bed; insomuch, that even canoes themselves, when loaded, cannot resist the stream, and are therefore sent empty to Lachine, where they meet the merchandize which they are to carry, and which is transported thither by land.* Lachine is about nine miles higher up

---

* *La Chine*, or China, has always been the point of departure, for the upper countries. It owes its name to the expeditions of M. de la Salle, which were fitted out at this place, for the discovery of a north-west passage to China.

the river, than Montréal, and is at the head of the
Sault de Saint-Louis, which is the highest of the
saults, falls, or *leaps*, in this part of the Saint-Lawrence.

On the third of August, I sent my canoes to Lachine; and, on the following morning, embarked
with them, for Michilimackinac. The river is here
so broad as to be denominated a lake, by the title
of Lake Saint-Louis; the prospect is wide and
cheerful; and the village has several well-built
houses.

In a short time, we reached the rapids and carrying place of Saint-Anne, two miles below the
upper end of the island of Montréal; and it is not
till after passing these, that the voyage may be properly said to be commenced. At Saint-Anne's,
the men go to confession, and, at the same time,
offer up their vows; for the saint, from which this
parish derives its name, and to whom its church is
dedicated, is the patroness of the Canadians, in all
their travels by water.

There is still a further custom to be observed, on
arriving at Saint-Anne's, and which is, that of dis-
tributing eight gallons of rum to each canoe (a gallon for each man) for consumption during the
voyage; nor is it less according to custom, to drink
the whole of this liquor upon the spot.—The saint,

therefore. and the priest, were no sooner dismissed, than a scene of intoxication began, in which my men surpassed, if possible, the drunken Indian, in singing, fighting, and the display of savage gesture and conceit. In the morning, we reloaded the canoes, and pursued our course, across the lake Des Deux Montagnes.

This lake, like that of Saint-Louis, is only a part of the estuary of the Outaouais, which here unites itself with the Saint-Lawrence, or rather, according to some, the Cataraqui ; for, with these, the Saint-Lawrence is formed by the confluence of the Cataraqui and Outaouais.*

At noon, we reached the Indian Mission of the Seminary of Saint-Sulpice, situate on the north bank of the lake, with its two villages, Algonquin and Iroquois, in each of which was reckoned an hundred souls. Here, we received a hospitable reception, and remained during two hours. I was informed, by one of the missionaries, that since the conquest of the country, the unrestrained introduction of spirituous liquors, at this place, which had not been allowed under the former government, had occasioned many outrages.

*This is the *Utawas* of some writers, the *Ottaway* of others, &c. &c. &c. It is also called the Grand River— *la Grande Riviere.*

At two o'clock in the afternoon, we prosecuted our voyage ; and, at sun-set, disembarked, and en-camped, at the foot of the Longue Sault.—There is a *Longue Sault*, both on this river, and on the Saint-Lawrence.

At ten leagues, above the island of Montréal, I passed the limits of the cultivated lands, on the north bank of the Outaouais. On the south, the farms are very few in number ; but the soil has every appearance of fertility.*

In ascending the Longue Sault, a distance of three miles, my canoes were three times unladen, and, together with their freight, carried on the shoulders of the *voyageurs*. The rocky carrying-places are not crossed, without danger of serious accidents, by men bearing heavy burdens.

The Longue Sault being passed, the Outaouais presented, on either side, only scenes of primitive forest, the common range of the deer, the wolf, the bear and the Indian. The current is here gentle. The lands upon the south are low, and, when I passed them, were overflowed ; but, on the northern side, the banks are dry and elevated, with much meadow-land at their feet. The grass,

---

* Numerous and thriving colonists are now enjoying that fertility.—1809.

in some places, was high.   Several islands are in
this part of the river.   Among the fish, of which
there are abundance, are cat-fish, of a large size.

At fourteen leagues, above the Longue Sault,
we reached a French fort, or trading-house, surrounded by a stockade.   Attached, was a small
garden, from which we procured some vegetables.
The house had no inhabitant.   At three leagues
further, is the mouth of the Hare-river, which descends from the north ; and here we passed another trading-house.   At a few leagues still higher,
on the south-bank, is the mouth of a river four
hundred yards wide, and which falls into the Outaouais perpendicularly, from the edge of a rock,
forty feet high.   The appearance of this fall, has
procured for it the name of the *rideau*, or, *cur-
tain ;* and hence the river itself is called the Rideau, or *Rivière du Rideau.*   The fall presented
itself to my view, with extraordinary beauty and
magnificence, and decorated with a variety of
colours.

Still ascending the Outaouais, at three leagues
from the fall of the Rideau, is that of La Grande
Chaudiere,* a phenomenon of a different aspect.
Here, on the north side of the river, is a deep chasm,
running across the channel, for about two hundred yards, from twenty-five to thirty feet in

La Grande Chaudière, *i. e.* the Great Kettle

depth, and without apparent outlet. In this receptacle, a large portion of the river falls perpendicularly, with a loud noise, and amid a cloud of
spray and vapour ; but, embellished, from time to
time, with the bright and gorgeous rainbow. The
river, at this place, is a mile in width. In the
rainy season, the depth of the fall is lessened, by
reason of the large quantity of water, which is received into the chasm, and which, for want, as it
would seem, of a sufficient drain, in part, fills
it up. At such times, an eddy, and an accumula-
tion of foam, at a particular part of the chasm, have
led me to suspect the existence of an opening beneath, through which the water finds a subterra-
nean passage. The rock, which forms the bed of
the river, appears to be split, in an oblique direction, from one shore to the other ; and the chasm,
on the north side, is only a more perfect breach.

The fall of La Grande Chaudière, is more than
twenty leagues above the Longue Sault. Its name
is justified, both by its form, and by the vapour, or
steam, which ascends from it. Above it, there are
several islands, of which the land is higher at the
upper, than at the lower extremities. The carrying-
place, is not more than a quarter of a mile in
length, over a smooth rock, and so near the fall,
that the men, in passing, are wetted by the spray.
From this carrying-place, to another, of rather
more length, called the Portage de la Chaudière,

and, sometimes, the Second Chaudière, is only three miles.

In this part of the voyage, I narrowly escaped a fatal accident. A thunder-gust having obliged us to make the shore, the men went into the woods, for shelter, while I remained in my canoe, under a covering of bark. The canoe had been intended to be sufficiently drawn aground ; but to my conster-nation, it was not long before, while thus left alone, I perceived it to be adrift, and going, with the current, toward La Grande Chaudiere. Hap-pily, I made a timely discovery of my situation ; and, getting out, in shallow water, was enabled, by the assistance of the men, who soon heard my call, to save my property, along with my life.

At twelve miles, from the second Portage de la Chaudière, there is a third Chaudière, but also called the Portage des Chênes. The name of this carrying-place is derived from the oak-trees, with which it abounds. It is half a mile in length, level, and of an agreeable aspect.

The bed of the river is here very broad, for a space of twelve leagues, or thirty-six miles ; and in this part of its course, it is called Lake des Chaudières, a name derived from the falls below. The current, in this place, is scarcely perceptible. The lands, on either side, are high,

and the soil is good. At the head of Lake des
Chaudières, is the Portage des Châts. The carrying-place is a high uneven rock, of difficult
access. The ridge of rock crosses the stream,
and occasions not only one, but numerous falls,
separated from each other by islands, and affording
a scene of very pleasing appearance. At the distance of a mile, seven openings present themselves
to the eye, along a line of two miles, which, at this
point, is the breadth of the river. At each opening,
is a fall of water, of about thirty feet in height, and
which, from the whiteness of its foam, might be
mistaken for a snow-bank. Above, for six miles,
there are many islands, between which, the current is strong. To overcome the difficulties of
this part of the navigation, the canoes first carry
one half of their loading, and, at a second trip,
the remainder.

Above the islands, the river is six miles in
width, and is called Lake des Châts. The lake,
so called, is thirty miles long. The lands about
the lake, are like those of Lake des Chaudières;
but, higher up, they are both high and rocky, and
covered with no other wood than spruce and
stunted pine.

While paddling against the gentle current of
Lake des Châts, we met several canoes of Indians,
returning, from their winter's hunt, to their village;

at the lake Des Deux Montagnes. I purchased some of their maple-sugar, and beaver-skins, in exchange for provisions. They wished for rum, which I declined to sell them ; but they behaved civilly, and we parted, as we had met, in a friendly manner. Before they left us, they inquired, of my men, whether or not I was an Englishman, and, being told that I was, they observed, that the English were mad, in their pursuit of beaver, since they could thus expose their lives for it ; " for," added they, " the Upper Indians will certainly kill him," meaning myself. These Indians had left their village before the surrender of Montréal, and I was the first Englishman they had seen.

In conversation with my men, I learned that the Algonquins, of the lake Des Deux Montagnes, of which description were the party that I had now met, claim all the lands on the Outaouais, as far as Lake Nipisingue ; and that these lands are subdivided, between their several families, upon whom they have devolved by inheritance. I was also informed, that they are exceedingly strict, as to the rights of property, in this regard, accounting an invasion of them an offence, sufficiently great to warrant the death of the invader.

We now reached the channels of the Grand Calumet, which lie amid numerous islands, and are about twenty miles in length. In this distance, there are four carrying-places,* besides three or four *décharges*,† or *discharges*, which are places where the merchandize only is carried, and are therefore distinguishable from *portages*, or carrying-places, where the canoe itself is taken out of the water, and transported on men's shoulders. The four carrying-places, included in the channels, are short; with the exception of one, called the Portage de la Montagne, at which, besides its length, there is an acclivity of a hundred feet.

On the 10th of July, we had reached the Portage du Grand Calumet, which is at the head of the channels of the same name, and which name is derived from the *pièrre à calumet*, or pipe-stone,‡ which here interrupts the river, occasioning a fall of water. This carrying-place is long and arduous, consisting in a high steep hill, over which the canoe cannot be carried by fewer than twelve men. The method of carrying the packages, or *pieces*, as they are called, is the same with that of the Indian women, and which, indeed, is not peculiar, even to them. One piece rests and hangs upon the shoulders, being suspended in a fillet, or forehead-band ; and upon this is laid a second, which usually falls

* Portage Dufort, &c.   †Décharge des Sables, &c.

‡ The *pièrre à calumet* is a compact lime-stone, yielding easily to the knife, and therefore employed for the bowls of tobacco-pipes, both by the Indians and Canadians.

into the hollow of the neck, and assists the head, in its support of the burden.

The ascent of this carrying-place is not more fatiguing, than the descent is dangerous ; and, in performing it, accidents too often occur, producing strains, ruptures, and injuries for life.*

The carrying-place, and the repairs of our canoes, which cost us a day, detained us till the 13th. It is usual for the canoes to leave the Grand Calumet in good repair ; the *rapids*, or shallow rocky parts of the channel (from which the canoes sustain the chief injury) being now passed, the current become gentle, and the carrying-places less frequent. The lands, above the carrying-places, and near the water, are low ; and, in the spring, entirely inundated.

On the morning of the 14th, we reached a trading fort, or house, surrounded by a stockade, which had been built by the French, and at which the quantity of peltries received was once not inconsiderable. For twenty miles below this house, the borders of the river are peculiarly well adapted to cultivation. From some Indians, who were en-

---

* A charitable fund is now established in Montreal, for the relief of disabled and decayed *voyageurs*.

camped near the house, I purchased fish, dried and fresh.

At the rapids, called Des Allumettes, are two short carrying-places, above which is the *rivière Creuse*,* twenty-six miles in length, where the water flows, with a gentle current, at the foot of a high, mountainous, barren and rocky country, on the north, and has a low and sandy soil on the south. On this southern side, is a remarkable point of sand, stretching far into the stream, and on which it is customary to baptize novices. Above the river Creuse, are the two carrying-places, of the length of half a mile each, called the Portages des Deux Joachins; and, at fifteen miles further, at the mouth of the river Du Moine, is another fort, or trading-house, where I found a small encampment of Indians, called Maskegons, and with whom I bartered several articles, for furs. They anxiously inquired, whether or not the English were in possession of the country below, and whether or not, if they were, they would allow traders to come to that trading-house; declaring, that their families must starve, unless they should be able to procure ammunition and other necessaries. I answered both these questions in the affirmative, at which they expressed much satisfaction.

* Called, by the English, *Deep-river.*

Above the Moine, are several strong and dangerous rapids, reaching to the Portage du Roche-Capitaine, a carrying-place of three quarters of a mile in length, mountainous, rocky, and wooded only with stunted pine-trees and spruce. Above this, is the Portage des Deux Rivières, so called, from the two small rivers by which it is intersected; and, higher still, are many rapids and shoals, called, by the Indians, *matawa*.* Here, the river, called, by the French, Petite Rivière, and, by the Indians, Matawa Sipi, falls into the Outaouais. We now left the latter of these rivers, and proceeded to ascend the Matawa.

* Mataouan (Matawan), *Charlevoix* ; Matawoen,—*Mackenzie's Voyages.*

CHAPTER III.

*Voyage from Montréal to Michilimackinac, conti-
nued. River Matawa. Lake Nipisingue.
Height of land. Nipisingues, Indians so called,—their nation and language. Animals of
the country. Mouth of the lake. Portage
de la Chaudière Française. Traces of the ancient
action of water, at high levels. River des Français. Embark on Lake Huron. Description of
its northern shores. Isle de la Cloche. Indian
Village. Missisakies. Indians persuaded that the
Author will be killed, at Michilimackinac, and
therefore demand a share of the pillage. Author
disguises himself, as a Canadian—in what that
disguise consists—meets frequent canoes, filled
with Indians, and is not recognized to be an Englishman. River Missisaki. Islands of Manitoualin.
Indians cultivate maize. River O'tossalon. Island
of Michilimackinac. Indian Village.*

OUR course, in ascending the Outaouais, had
been west-north-west; but, on entering the Matawa,
our faces were turned to the south-west. This
latter river is computed to be fourteen leagues

in length. In the widest parts, it is a hundred yards broad, and in others not more than fifty. In ascending it, there are fourteen carrying-places and discharges, of which some are extremely difficult. Its banks are almost two continuous rocks, with scarcely earth enough for the burial of a dead body. I saw Indian graves, if graves they might be called, where the corpse was laid upon the bare rock, and covered with stones. In the side of a hill, on the north side of the river, there is a curious cave, concerning which marvellous tales are related, by the *voyageurs*. Mosquitoes, and a minute species of black fly, abound on this river, the latter of which are still more troublesome than the former. To obtain a respite from their vexations, we were obliged, at the carrying-places, to make fires, and stand in the smoke.

On the 26th of August, we reached the Portages à la Vase, three in number, and each two miles in length. Their name describes the boggy ground of which they consist. In passing one of them, we saw many beaver-houses and dams; and by breaking one of the dams, we let off water enough to float our canoes down a small stream, which would not otherwise have been navigable. These carrying-places, and the intermediate navigation, brought us, at length, to the head of a small river, which falls into Lake Nipisingue. We had now passed the country, of which the streams fall north-eastward, into the Outaouais, and entered that from which they flow, in a contrary direction, toward Lake Huron. On one side of the *height of land*, which is the reciprocal boundary of these regions, we had left Lake aux Tourtres and the river Matawa ; and before us, on the other, was Lake Nipisingue. The banks of the little river, by which we descended into the lake, and more especially as we approached the lake, were of an exceedingly delightful appearance, covered with high grass, and affording an extensive prospect. Both the lake and river abound in black bass, sturgeon, pike and other fish. Among the pike, is to be included the species, called, by the Indians, *masquinongé*. In two hours, with the assistance of an Indian, we took as much fish as all the party could eat.

Lake Nipisingue is distant two hundred leagues from Montréal. Its circumference is said to measure one hundred and fifty miles, and its depth is sufficient for vessels of any burden. On our voyage, along its eastern banks, we met some canoes of Indians, who said they lived on the north-western side. My men informed me that they were Nipisingues, a name which they derive from the lake. Their language is a dialect of the Algonquin ; and, by nation, they are a mixture of Chipeways and Maskegons. They had a large quantity of furs, part of which I purchased. The animals, which the country affords them, are the beaver, marten, bear and *o'tic*, *a'tic*, or, *caribou*, a species of deer, by some called the *rein-deer*. They wished for rum, but I avoided selling or giving them any.

Leaving the Indians, we proceeded to the mouth of the lake, at which is the carrying-place of La Chaudière Française,* a name, part of which it has obtained from the holes, in the rock over which we passed; and which holes, being of the kind which is known to be formed by water, with the assistance of pebbles, demonstrate that it has not always been dry, as at present it is ; but the phenomenon is not peculiar to this spot, the same being observable, at almost every carrying-place on the Outaouais. At the height of a hundred feet above the river, I commonly found pebbles, worn into a round form, like those upon the beach below. Everywhere, the water appears to have subsided from its ancient levels ; and imagination may anticipate an era, at which even the banks of Newfoundland will be left bare.

The southern shores of Lake Nipisingue are rocky, and only thinly covered with pine-trees and spruce, both, as in several instances already mentioned, of a small stature. The carrying-place of La Chaudière Francaise is at the head of the river Des

---

* Or, *la Chaudiere des Français.*

Français, and where the water first descends from
the level of Lake Nipisingue toward that of Lake
Huron.   This it does not reach till it has passed
down many rapids, full of danger to the canoes
and the men, after which it enters Lake Huron by several arms, flowing through each, as through a mill-
race.   The river Des Français is twenty leagues in
length, and has many islands in its channel. Its banks
are uniformly of rock. Among the carrying-places, at
which we successively arrived, are the Portage des
Pins, or, du Pin ; de la Grande Faucille ;* de la
Petite Faucille; and du Sault du Recolet.† Near the
mouth of the river, a meadow, called La Prairie
des Français, varies, for a short space, the rocky
surface, which so generally prevails ; and, on this
spot, we encamped, and repaired our canoes. The
carrying-places were now all passed, and what remained was, to cross the billows of Lake Huron,
which lay stretched across our horizon, like an
ocean.

On the thirty-first day of August, we entered the
lake, the waves running high, from the south, and
breaking over numerous rocks.   At first, I thought
the prospect alarming ; but the canoes rode on the

---

* *Faucille*, Fr. a sickle.

† So called, perhaps, on account of the resemblance of this
Sault to that of the Sault du Recolet, between the islands of
Montréal and Jesus, and which has its name from the death of
a Recolet, or Franciscan friar, who was there drowned.

water with the ease of a sea-bird, and my apprehensions ceased. We passed Point de Grondines, so called, from the perpetual noise of the water among the rocks. Many of these rocks are sunken, and not without danger, when the wind, as at this time it was, is from the south.

We coasted along many small islands, or rather rocks, of more or less extent, either wholly bare, or very scantily covered with scrub pine-trees. All the land to the northward is of the same description, as high as Cha'ba'bou'an'ing', where verdure reappears.

On the following day, we reached an island, called La Cloche, because there is here a rock, standing on a plain, which, being struck, rings like a bell.

I found the island inhabited by a large village of Indians, whose behaviour was at first full of civility and kindness. I bartered away some small articles among them, in exchange for fish and dried meat; and we remained upon friendly terms, till, discovering that I was an Englishman, they told my men, that the Indians, at Michilimackinac, would not fail to kill me, and that, therefore, they had a right to a share of the pillage. Upon this principle, as they said, they demanded a keg of rum, adding, that if not given them, they would proceed to take it.   I judged it prudent to comply ; on condition, however, that I should experience, at this place, no further molestation.

The condition was not unfaithfully observed ; but the repeated warnings which I had now received, of sure destruction at Michilimackinac, could not but oppress my mind.   I could not even yield myself, without danger, to the course suggested by my fears ; for my provisions were nearly exhausted, and to return, was, therefore, almost impracticable.

The hostility of the Indians was exclusively against the English.   Between them, and my Canadian attendants, there appeared the most cordial good will.   This circumstance suggested one means of escape, of which, by the advice of my friend, Campion, I resolved to attempt availing myself ; and which was, that of putting on the dress, usually worn by such of the Canadians as pursue the trade into which I had entered, and assimilating myself, as much as I was able, to their appearance and manners.   To this end, I laid aside my English clothes, and covered myself only with a cloth, passed about the middle; a shirt, hanging loose; a molton, or blanket coat ; and a large, red, milled worsted cap.   The next thing was to smear my face and hands, with dirt and grease ; and, this done, I took the place of one of my men, and, when

Indians approached, used the paddle, with as much skill as I possessed. I had the satisfaction to find, that my disguise enabled me to pass several canoes, without attracting the smallest notice.

In this manner, I pursued my voyage to the mouth, or rather mouths, of the Missisaki, a river which descends from the north, and of which the name imports, that it has several mouths, or outlets. From this river, all the Indians, inhabiting the north side of Lake Huron, are called Missisakies. There is here a plentiful sturgeon-fishery, by which those, that resort to it, are fed during the summer months. On our voyage, we met several Missisakies, of whom we bought fish, and from whose stock we might easily have filled all our canoes.

From the Missisaki, which is on the north shore of Lake Huron, to Michilimackinac, which is on the south, is reckoned thirty leagues. The lake, which here approaches Lake Superior, is now contracted in its breadth, as well as filled with islands. From the mouth of the river Des Français, to the Missisaki, is reckoned fifty leagues, with many islands along the route. The lands everywhere, from the island of La Cloche, are poor ; with the exception of those of the island of

Manitoualin, a hundred miles in length,* where
they are generally good.   On all the islands, the
Indians cultivate small quantities of maize.

From the Missisaki, we proceeded to the O'tossalon,† and thence across the lake, making one
island after another, at intervals of from two to
three leagues. The lake, as far as it could be seen,
tended to the westward, and became less and less
broad.

The first land, which we made, on the south
shore, was that called Point du Détour, after
which, we passed the island called Isle aux
Outardes, and then, leaving on the right, the
deep bay of Boutchitaouy came to the island of
Michilimackinac, distant, from Isle aux Outardes,

---

* The *Isle Manitoualin* was formerly so described.   It is
now known, that there is no island in Lake Huron, of a hundred miles in length, and that the *Manitoualin* are a chain
of islands.   The French writers on Canada, speak of the
Isle Manitoualin, as inhabited, in their time, by the Ami-
koues (Amicways, Amicawac), whom they called a family
(and sometimes a nation), deriving its origin from the Great
Beaver, a personage of mythological importance. The name
Manitoualin, implies the residence of *Manitoes*, or genii,
a distinction very commonly attributed to the islands, and
sometimes to the shores, of Lakes Huron and Superior, and
of which, further examples will present themselves, in the
course of these pages.

Also written, *Tessalon*, *Thessalon*, and *des Tessalons*

three leagues. On our way, a sudden squall reduced us to the point of throwing over the cargoes
of our canoes, to save the latter from filling; but
the wind subsided, and we reached the island in
safety.

The land, in the centre of this island, is high,
and its form somewhat resembles that of a turtle's
back. Mackinac, or Mickinac, signifies a *turtle*,
and *michi* (*mishi*), or *missi*, signifies *great*, as it
does also, *several*, or *many*. The common interpretation, of the word, *Michilimackinac*, is the Great
Turtle. It is from this island, that the fort, commonly known by the name of Michilimackinac,
has obtained its appellation.

On the island, as I had been previously taught
to expect, there was a village of Chipeways, said to
contain a hundred warriors. Here, I was fearful of
discovery, and consequent ill-treatment; but after
inquiring the news, and, particularly, whether or
not any Englishman was coming to Michilimackinac, they suffered us to pass, uninjured. One
man, indeed, looked at me, laughed, and pointed
me out to another. This was enough to give me
some uneasiness; but, whatever was the singularity
he perceived in me, both he and his friend retired,
without suspecting me to be an Englishman.

CHAPTER IV.

Fort Michilimackinac. Chipeways, of the Island of Michilimackinac—their appearance—demeanour—and treatment of the Author. Otawas, of the village of L'Arbre Croche—their condition—their treatment of the Author and others. Arrival of a British garrison.

LEAVING, as speedily as possible, the island of Michilimackinac, I crossed the strait, and landed at the fort, of the same name. The distance, from the island, is about two leagues. I landed, at four o'clock in the afternoon.

Here, I put the entire charge of my effects into the hands of my assistant, Campion, between whom and myself it had been previously agreed, that he should pass for the proprietor; and my men were instructed to conceal the fact, that I was an Englishman.

Campion, soon found a house, to which I retired, and where I hoped to remain in privacy; but the men soon betrayed my secret, and I was visited by the inhabitants, with great show of civility.

They assured me, that I could not stay at Michilimackinac without the most imminent risk; and
strongly recommended, that I should lose no time,
in making my escape, to Détroit.

Though language, like this, could not but increase my uneasiness, it did not shake my determination, to remain with my property, and encounter
the evils with which I was threatened; and my
spirits were in some measure sustained by the sentiments of Campion, in this regard; for he declared
his belief, that the Canadian inhabitants of the fort
were more hostile than the Indians, as being jealous
of English traders, who, like myself, were penetra-
ting into the country.

Fort Michilimackinac was built by order of
the governor-general of Canada, and garrisoned
with a small number of militia, who, having families, soon became less soldiers than settlers. Most
of those, whom I found in the fort, had originally
served in the French army.

The fort stands on the south side of the strait
which is between Lake Huron and Lake Michigan.
It has an area of two acres, and is enclosed with
pickets of cedar-wood;* and it is so near the water's
edge, that, when the wind is in the west, the waves

* Thuya occidentalis.

break against the stockade. On the bastions, are two small pieces of brass English cannon, taken some years since, by a party of Canadians, who went on a plundering expedition, against the posts of Hudson's Bay, which they reached by the route of the river Churchill.

Within the stockade, are thirty houses, neat in their appearance, and tolerably commodious ; and a church, in which mass is celebrated, by a jesuit missionary. The number of families may be nearly equal to that of the houses ; and their subsistence is derived from the Indian traders, who assemble here, in their voyages to and from Montréal. Michilimackinac is the place of deposit, and point of departure, between the upper countries and the lower. Here, the outfits are prepared for the countries of Lake Michigan and the Missisipi, Lake Superior and the north-west ; and here, the returns, in furs, are collected, and embarked for Montréal.

I was not released from the visits and admonitions of the inhabitants of the fort, before I received the equivocal intelligence, that the whole band of Chipeways, from the island of Michilimackinac, was arrived, with the intention of paying me a visit.

There was, in the fort, one Farley, an interpreter, lately in the employ of the French commandant.

He had married a Chipeway woman, and was
said to possess great influence over the nation
to which his wife belonged. Doubtful, as to the
kind of visit which I was about to receive, I sent
for this interpreter, and requested, first, that he
would have the kindness to be present at the interview, and, secondly, that he would inform me of
the intentions of the band. M. Farley agreed to
be present; and, as to the object of the visit, replied,
that it was consistent with uniform custom, that a
stranger, on his arrival, should be waited upon, and
welcomed, by the chiefs of the nation, who, on
their part, always gave a small present, and always
expected a large one ; but, as to the rest, declared
himself unable to answer for the particular views of
the Chipeways, on this occasion, I being an Englishman, and the Indians having made no treaty
with the English. He thought that there might
be danger, the Indians having protested that they
would not suffer an Englishman to remain in their
part of the country.—This information was far
from agreeable ; but there was no resource, except in fortitude and patience.

At two o'clock in the afternoon, the Chipeways
came to my house, about sixty in number, and head-
ed by Mina'va'va'na', their chief. They walked in
single file, each with his tomahawk in one hand,
and scalping-knife in the other. Their bodies
were naked, from the waist upward ; except in a

6

few examples, where blankets were thrown loosely over the shoulders. Their faces were painted with charcoal, worked up with grease; their bodies, with white clay, in patterns of various fancies. Some had feathers thrust through their noses, and their heads decorated with the same.---It is unnecessary to dwell on the sensations with which I beheld the approach of this uncouth, if not frightful assemblage.

The chief entered first; and the rest followed, without noise. On receiving a sign from the former, the latter seated themselves on the floor.

Minavavana appeared to be about fifty years of age. He was six feet in height, and had, in his countenance, an indescribable mixture of good and evil.---Looking stedfastly at me, where I sat in ceremony, with an interpreter on either hand, and several Canadians behind me, he entered at the same time into conversation with Campion, inquiring how long it was since I left Montréal, and observing, that the English, as it would seem, were brave men, and not afraid of death, since they dared to come, as I had done, fearlessly among their enemies.

The Indians now gravely smoked their pipes, while I inwardly endured the tortures of suspense.--- At length, the pipes being finished, as well as a

long pause, by which they were succeeded, Minavavana, taking a few strings of wampum in his
hand, began the following speech :

   " Englishman, it is to you that I speak, and I
" demand your attention !

   " Englishman, you know that the French king
" is our father. He promised to be such ; and we,
" in return, promised to be his children.---This
" promise we have kept.

   " Englishman, it is you that have made war
" with this our father.   You are his enemy ; and
" how, then, could you have the boldness to venture
" among us, his children?---You know that his ene-
" mies are ours.

   " Englishman, we are informed, that our father,
" the king of France, is old and infirm ; and that
" being fatigued, with making war upon your nation,
" he is fallen asleep. During his sleep, you have taken
" advantage of him, and possessed yourselves of Ca-
" nada.   But, his nap is almost at an end.   I think
" I hear him already stirring, and inquiring for
" his children, the Indians ;---and, when he does
" awake, what must become of you? He will destroy
" you utterly !

" Englishman, although you have conquered
" the French, you have not yet conquered us ! We
" are not your slaves. These lakes, these woods and
" mountains, were left to us by our ancestors. They
" are our inheritance; and we will part with them to
" none.   Your nation supposes that we, like the
" white people, cannot live without bread---and
" pork---and beef ! But, you ought to know, that
" He, the Great Spirit and Master of Life, has provi-
" ded food for us, in these spacious lakes, and on
" these woody mountains.

" Englishman, our father, the king of France,
" employed our young men to make war upon your
" nation. In this warfare, many of them have been
" killed; and it is our custom to retaliate, until such
" time as the spirits of the slain are satisfied. But,
" the spirits of the slain are to be satisfied in either of
" two ways ; the first is by the spilling of the blood
" of the nation by which they fell; the other, by *co-*
" *vering the bodies of the dead*, and thus allaying the
" resentment of their relations. This is done by
" making presents.

" Englishman, your king has never sent us any
" presents, nor entered into any treaty with us, where-
" fore he and we are still at war ; and, until he does
" these things, we must consider that we have no
" other father, nor friend, among the white men, than
" the king of France ; but, for you, we have taken

" into consideration, that you have ventured your
" life among us, in the expectation that we should
" not molest you.   You do not come armed, with
" an intention to make war; you come in peace, to
" trade with us, and supply us with necessaries, of
" which we are in much want. We shall regard you,
" therefore, as a brother; and you may sleep tranquil-
" ly, without fear of the Chipeways.----As a token of
" our friendship, we present you with this pipe, to
" smoke."

As Minavavana uttered these words, an Indian
presented me with a pipe, which, after I had drawn
the smoke three times, was carried to the chief,
and after him to every person in the room.   This
ceremony ended, the chief arose, and gave me his
hand, in which he was followed by all the rest.

Being again seated, Minavavana requested that
his young men might be allowed to taste what he
called my *English milk* (meaning *rum*)---observing,
that it was long since they had tasted any, and that
they were very desirous to know, whether or not
there were any difference between the English milk
and the French.

My adventure, on leaving Fort William-Augustus, had left an impression on my mind, which made
me tremble when Indians asked for rum; and I
would therefore willingly have excused myself in
this particular : but, being informed that it was

customary to comply with the request, and withal satisfied with the friendly declarations which I had received, I promised to give them a small cask, at parting.

After this, by the aid of my interpreter, I made a reply to the speech of Minavavana, declaring that it was the good character, which I had heard of the Indians, that had alone emboldened me to come among them ; that their late father, the king of France, had surrendered Canada to the king of England, whom they ought now to regard as their father, and who would be as careful of them as the other had been ; that I had come to furnish them with necessaries, and that their good treatment of me would be an encouragement to others.—They appeared satisfied with what I said, repeating *eh !* (an expression of approbation) after hearing each particular. I had prepared a present, which I now gave them, with the utmost good will. At their departure, I distributed a small quantity of rum.

Relieved, as I now imagined myself, from all occasion of anxiety, as to the treatment which I was to experience, from the Indians, I assorted my goods, and hired Canadian interpreters and clerks, in whose care I was to send them into Lake Michigan, and the river Saint-Pièrre, in the country of the Nadowessies; into Lake Superior, among the Chipeways, and to the Grand Portage, for the north-west.   Every thing was ready for their departure, when new dangers sprung up, and threatened to overwhelm me.

At the entrance of Lake Michigan, and at about twenty miles to the west of Fort Michilimackinac, is the village of L'Arbre Croche, inhabited by a band of Otawas, boasting of two hundred and fifty fighting men.   L'Arbre Croche is the seat of the Jesuit mission of Saint Ignace de Michilimackinac, and the people are partly baptized, and partly not.   The missionary resides on a farm, attached to the mission, and situated between the village and the fort, both of which are under his care.   The Otawas of L'Arbre Croche, who, when compared with the Chipeways, appear to be much advanced in civilization, grow maize, for the market of Michilimackinac, where this commodity is depended upon, for provisioning the canoes.

The new dangers, which presented themselves, came from this village of Otawas.   Every thing, as I have said, was in readiness, for the departure of my goods, when accounts arrived of its approach ; and shortly after, two hundred warriors entered the fort, and billeted themselves in the several houses, among the Canadian inhabitants. The next morning, they assembled in the house which was built for the commandant, or governor, and ordered the attendance of myself, and of two other merchants, still later from Montréal, namely, Messrs. Stanley Goddard, and Ezekiel Solomons.

After our entering the council-room, and taking our seats, one of the chiefs commenced an address : " Englishmen," said he, " we, the Ota-
" was, were some time since informed of your ar-
" rival in this country, and of your having brought
" with you the goods of which we have need.   At
" this news, we were greatly pleased, believing, that
" through your assistance, our wives and children
" would be enabled to pass another winter ; but,
" what was our surprise, when, a few days ago, we
" were again informed, that the goods which, as we
" had expected, were intended for us were, on the
" eve of departure, for distant countries, of which
" some are inhabited by our enemies !   These ac-
" counts being spread, our wives and children came
" to us, crying, and desiring that we should go to
" the fort, to learn, with our own ears, their truth
" or falsehood. We accordingly embarked, almost
" naked, as you see ; and on our arrival here, we
" have inquired into the accounts, and found them
" true. We see your canoes ready to depart, and
" find your men engaged for the Missisipi, and
" other distant regions.

" Under these circumstances, we have consider-
" ed the affair ; and you are now sent for, that you
" may hear our determination, which is, that you

" that you shall give to each of our men, young
" and old, merchandize and ammunition, to the
" amount of fifty beaver-skins, on credit, and for
" which I have no doubt of their paying you in
" the summer, on their return from their winter-
" ing."

A compliance with this demand would have
stripped me and my fellow-merchants of all our
merchandize ; and, what rendered the affair still
more serious, we even learned that these Otawas
were never accustomed to pay for what they received on credit. In reply, therefore, to the speech
which we had heard, we requested that the demand
contained in it might be diminished ; but we were
answered, that the Otawas had nothing further
to say, except that they would allow till the next
day for reflection ; after which, if compliance was
not given, they would make no further application,
but take into their own hands the property, which
they already regarded as their own, as having been
brought into their country, before the conclusion
of any peace, between themselves and the English.

We now returned, to consider of our situation ;
and, in the evening, Farley, the interpreter, paid us
a visit, and assured us that it was the intention of
the Otawas to put us, that night, to death. He advised us, as our only means of safety, to comply
with the demands which had been made ; but, we

7

suspected our informant of a disposition to prey
upon our fears, with a view to induce us to abandon
the Indian trade, and resolved, however this might
be, rather to stand on the defensive, than submit.
We trusted to the house, in which I lived, as a fort;
and armed ourselves, and about thirty of our men,
with muskets. Whether or not the Otawas ever
intended violence, we never had an opportunity of
knowing; but the night passed quietly.

Early the next morning, a second council was
held, and the merchants were again summoned to
attend. Believing that every hope of resistance
would be lost, should we commit our persons into
the hands of our enemies, we sent only a refusal. There was none without, in whom we had
any confidence, except Campion. From him we
learned, from time to time, whatever was rumoured
among the Canadian inhabitants, as to the designs
of the Otawas; and, from him, toward sunset, we
received the gratifying intelligence, that a detachment of British soldiery, sent to garrison Michilimackinac, was distant only five miles, and would
enter the fort early the next morning.

Near at hand, however, as relief was reported to
be, our anxiety could not but be great; for a long
night was to be passed, and our fate might be deci-
ded before the morning. To increase our apprehensions, about midnight we were informed, that

the Otawas were holding a council, at which no
white man was permitted to be present, Farley
alone excepted ; and him we suspected, and afterward positively knew, to be our greatest enemy.
We, on our part, remained all night upon the
alert ; but, at day-break, to our surprize and joy,
we saw the Otawas preparing to depart. By sunrise, not a man of them was left in the fort ; and,
indeed the scene was altogether changed. The
inhabitants, who, while the Otawas were present,
had avoided all connection with the English traders, now came with congratulations. They related, that the Otawas had proposed to them, that if
joined by the Canadians, they would march, and
attack the troops which were known to be advancing on the fort ; and they added, that it was their
refusal which had determined the Otawas to depart.

At noon, three hundred troops, of the sixtieth
regiment, under the command of Lieutenant Lesslie,
marched into the fort ; and this arrival dissipated all
our fears, from whatever source derived. After a
few days, detachments were sent into the Bay des
Puans, by which is the route to the Missisipi, and
at the mouth of the Saint-Joseph, which leads to the
Illinois. The Indians, from all quarters, came to pay
their respects to the commandant ; and the merchants dispatched their canoes, though it was now
the middle of September, and therefore somewhat
late in the season.

CHAPTER V.

Of the particular mode of victualling the canoes, at
Michilimackinac—and its importance to the trade
in furs. Winter amusements at Michilimack-
inac—hunting—fishing—trout-fishing. Exorbi-
tant price of grain and beef. Furs the circulating
medium—their nominal value. White-fish—and
mode of taking it. Anecdote of a Chipeway
Chief. Depth of Snow—return of Spring.

THE village of L'Arbre Croche supplies, as I
have said, the maize, or *Indian corn*, with which the
canoes are victualled. This species of grain is prepared for use, by boiling it in a strong lie, after which
the husk may be easily removed; and it is next
mashed and dried. In this state, it is soft and
friable, like rice. The allowance, for each man,
on the voyage, is a quart a day; and a bushel, with
two pounds of prepared fat, is reckoned to be a
month's subsistence. No other allowance is made,
of any kind; not even of salt; and bread is never
thought of. The men, nevertheless, are healthy,
and capable of performing their heavy labour.
This mode of victualling is essential to the

trade, which being pursued at great distances, and in vessels so small as canoes, will not admit of the use of other food. If the men were to be supplied with bread and pork, the canoes could not carry a sufficiency for six months ; and the ordinary duration of the voyage is not less than fourteen. The difficulty, which would belong to an attempt to reconcile any other men, than Canadians, to this fare, seems to secure to them, and their employers, the monopoly of the fur-trade.

The sociable disposition of the commandant enabled us to pass the winter, at Michilimackinac, in a manner as agreeable as circumstances would permit. The amusements consisted chiefly in shooting, hunting and fishing. The neighbouring woods abounded in *partridges** and hares, the latter of which is white in winter ; and the lake is filled with fish, of which the most celebrated are trout, white-fish and sturgeon.

Trout are taken by making holes in the ice, in which are set lines and baits. These are often left for many days together, and in some places at the depth of fifty fathoms; for, the trout having swallowed the bait, remains fast, and alive, till taken up.

* In North-America, there is no *partridge ;* but the name is given to more than one species of grouse. The birds, here intended, are red grouse.

This fish, which is found of the weight of from ten to sixty pounds, and upward, constitutes the principal food of the inhabitants. When this fails, they have recourse to maize, but this is very expensive. I bought more than a hundred bushels, at forty livres per bushel. Money is rarely received or paid at Michilimackinac, the circulating medium consisting in furs and peltries. In this exchange, a pound of beaver-skin is reckoned at sixty sols; an otter-skin, at six livres; and marten-skins, at thirty sols, each. This is only one half of the real value of the furs; and it is therefore always agreed, to pay either in furs at their actual price at the fort, or in cash, to double the amount, as reckoned in furs.

At the same time that I paid the price, which I have mentioned, for maize, I paid at the rate of a dollar per pound for the tallow, or prepared fat, to mix with it. The meat itself was at the same price. The jesuit missionary killed an ox, which he sold by the quarter, taking the weight of the meat in beaver-skin. Beaver-skin, as just intimated, was worth a dollar per pound.

These high prices of grain and beef led me to be very industrious in fishing. I usually set twenty lines, and visited them daily, and often found, at every visit, fish enough to feed a hundred men. White-fish, which exceed the trout, as a delicious

and nutritive food, are here in astonishing numbers. In shape, they somewhat resemble the shad ;
but their flavour is perhaps above all comparison
whatever. Those, who live on them for months
together, preserve their relish to the end. This
cannot be said of the trout.

The white-fish is taken in nets, which are set under
the ice. To do this, several holes are made in the ice,
each at such distance from that behind it, as that it
may, be reached, under the ice, by the end of a pole.
A line, of sixty fathoms in length, is thus conveyed from hole to hole, till it is extended to the length
desired. This done, the pole is taken out, and
with it one end of the line, to which the end is then
fastened. The line being now drawn back, by an
assistant, who holds the opposite extremity, the net
is brought under, and a large stone is made fast to
the sinking-line, at each end, and let down to the
bottom ; and the net is spread in the water, by
lighters on its upper edge, sinkers on its lower, in
the usual manner. The fish, running against the
net, entangle their gills in the meshes, and are thus
detained till taken up. White-fish is used as a
bait for trout. They are much smaller than the
trout, but usually weigh, at Michilimackinac, from
three to seven pounds.

During the whole winter, very few Indians visited the fort ; but, two families, one of which was

that of a chief, had their lodges on a river, five leagues below us, and occasionally brought bea- ver-flesh for sale.

The chief was warmly attached to the English. He had been taken prisoner by Sir William John- son, at the siege of Fort Niagara; and had received, from that intelligent officer, his liberty, the medal usually presented to a chief, and the British flag. Won, by these unexpected acts of kindness, he had returned to Michilimackinac, full of praises of the English, and hoisting his flag over his lodge. This latter demonstration of his partiality had nearly cost him his life ; his lodge was broken down, and his flag torn to pieces. The pieces he care- fully gathered up, and preserved with pious care ; and, whenever he came to the fort, he drew them forth, and exhibited them. On these occasions, it grew into a custom, to give him as much liquor as he said was necessary to make him cry, over the misfortune of losing his flag. The commandant would have given him another ; but he thought that he could not accept it without danger.

The greatest depth of snow, throughout the season, was three feet. On the second day of April, the ice on the lake broke up, and the navi- gation was resumed ; and we immediately began to receive, from the Indians around us, large sup- plies of wild-fowl.

CHAPTER VI.

Voyage from Michilimackinac to the Sault de Sainte-Marie. Description of the Fort. White-fish—singular method of taking them. Village of Chipeways. O'pimittish Ininiwac, Wood-Indians, or Gens de Terres—their condition—mode of life—food and clothing. Summer. The Fort receives a Garrison from Michilimackinac.

BEING desirous of visiting the Sault de Sainte-Marie, I left Michilimackinac on the 15th of May, in a canoe. The Sault de Sainte-Marie is distant from Michilimackinac thirty leagues, and lies in the strait which separates Lake Huron from Lake Superior.

Having passed Le Détour, a point of land at the entrance of the strait, our course lay among numerous islands, some of which are twenty miles in length. We ascended the *rapid* of Miscoutinsaki, a spot well adapted for mill-seats, and above which is the mouth of the river of the same name. The lands, on the south shore of this river, are excel-

8

lent.   The lake is bordered by meadows, and, at a short distance back, are groves of sugar-maple. From this river, to the Sault de Sainte-Marie, is one continued meadow.

On the 19th, I reached the Sault.   Here was a stockaded fort, in which, under the French govern· ment, there was kept a small garrison, commanded by an officer, who was called *the governor*, but was in fact a clerk, who managed the Indian trade here, on government account.   The houses were four in number; of which the first was the governor's, the second the interpreter's, and the other two, which were the smallest, had been used for bar- racks.   The only family was that of M. Cadotte, the interpreter, whose wife was a Chipeway.

The fort is seated on a beautiful plain, of about two miles in circumference, and covered with luxuriant grass ; and, within sight, are the *rapids* in the strait, distant half a mile.   The width of the strait, or river, is about half a mile.   The *portage*, or carrying-place, commences at the fort.   The banks are rocky, and allow only a narrow foot-path over them.   Canoes, half loaded, ascend, on the south side, and the other half of the load is carried on men's shoulders.

These *rapids* are beset with rocks of the most dangerous description ; and yet they are the scene of a fishery, in which all their dangers are braved, and mastered with singular expertness.   They are full of white-fish, much larger and more excellent than those of Michilimackinac, and which are found here during the greater part of the season, weighing, in general, from six pounds to fifteen.

The method of taking them is this: each canoe carries two men, one of whom steers with a paddle, and the other is provided with a pole, ten feet in length, and at the end of which is affixed a scoop-net.   The steersman sets the canoe from the eddy of one rock to that of another; while the fisherman, in the prow, who sees, through the pellucid element, the prey of which he is in pursuit, dips his net, and sometimes brings up, at every succeeding dip, as many as it can contain.   The fish are often crowded together in the water, in great numbers; and a skilful fisherman, in autumn, will take five hundred in two hours.

This fishery is of great moment to the surrounding Indians, whom it supplies with a large proportion of their winter's provision; for, having taken the fish, in the manner described, they cure them, by drying in the smoke, and lay them up in large quantities.

There is at present a village of Chipeways, of fifty warriors, seated at this place ; but the inhabitants reside here during the summer only, going westward, in the winter, to hunt.   The village was anciently much more populous.

At the south are also seen a few of the wandering *O'pimittish Ininiwac*, literally, Men of the Woods, and otherwise called Wood-Indians, and *Gens de Terres*—a peaceable and inoffensive race, but less conversant with some of the arts of first necessity than any of their neighbours. They have no villages ; and their lodges are so rudely fashioned, as to afford them but very inadequate protection against inclement skies.   The greater part of their year is spent in travelling from place to place, in search of food.   The animal, on which they chiefly depend, is the hare.   This they take in springes.   Of the skin, they make coverings, with much ingenuity, cutting it into narrow strips, and weaving these into a cloth, of the shape of a blanket, and of a quality very warm and agreeable.

The pleasant situation of the fort, and still more the desire of learning the Chipeway language, led me to resolve on wintering in it.   In the family of M. Cadotte, no other language than the Chipeway was spoken.

During the summer, the weather was sometimes exceedingly hot. Mosquitoes and black-flies were so numerous as to be a heavy counterpoise to the pleasure of hunting. Pigeons were in great plenty; the stream supplied our drink; and sickness was unknown.

In the course of the season, a small detachment of troops, under the command of Lieutenant Jemette, arrived to garrison the fort.

CHAPTER VII.

An abundant supply of Fish is obtained at the Fort— but improvidently managed. The Governor's House, and others, burnt, together with all the provisions of the Garrison. The Soldiers, to avoid famine, are re-embarked for Michilimackinac. Method of taking Trout with spears. The Author accompanies the Commandant and Interpreter, on a Journey, by land, to Michilimackinac. The party is twice in danger of starving—it reaches Michilimackinac. Author returns to the Sault. Account of the Snow-Shoe Evil. Bay of Boutchitaouy. Maple-sugar making. Author returns to Michilimackinac.

IN the beginning of October, the fish, as is usual, was in great abundance at the Sault ; and, by the fifteenth day of the month, I had myself taken upward of five hundred. These, I caused to be dried, in the customary manner, by suspending them, in pairs, head downward, on long poles, laid horizontally, for that purpose, and supported by two stakes, driven into the ground at either end. The fish are frozen the first night after they are taken ; and, by the aid of the severe cold of the winter, they are thus preserved, in a state perfectly fit for use, even till the month of April.

Others were not less successful than myself; and several canoe-loads of fish were exported to Michili-mackinac, our commanding officer being unable to believe that his troops would have need to live on fish during the winter; when, as he flattered him-self, a regular supply of venison and other food would reach the garrison, through the means of the In-dians, whose services he proposed to purchase, out of the large funds of liquor which were sub-ject to his orders.

But, all these calculations were defeated, by the arrival of a very serious misfortune. At one o'clock, in the morning of the twenty-second day of December, I was awakened by an alarm of fire, which was actually raging in the houses of the commandant and others. On arriving at the commandant's, I found that this officer was still within side; and, being acquainted with the win-dow of the room in which he slept, I procured it to be broken in, in time for his escape. I was also so fortunate as to save a small quantity of gunpow-der, only a few moments before the fire reached all the remainder. A part of the stockade, all the houses, M. Cadotte's alone excepted, all the provi-sions of the troops, and a considerable part of our fish, were burnt.

On consultation, the next day, it was agreed, that
the only means which remained, at this late period
of the season, to preserve the garrison from famine, was that of sending it back to Michilimackinac. This was itself an undertaking of some peril;
for, had the ice prevented their reaching the place
of destination, starving would have become as
inevitable elsewhere, as it threatened to be at the
Sault de Sainte-Marie. The soldiers embarked,
and happily reached Michilimackinac on the thirty-
first day of the month. On the very next morning, the navigation was wholly closed.

The commandant, and all the rest, now lived
in one small house, subsisting only by hunting
and fishing. The woods afforded us some hares
and partridges, and we took large trout with
the spear. In order to spear trout under the
ice, holes being first cut, of two yards in circumference, cabins of about two feet in height,
are built over them, of small branches of trees;
and these are further covered with skins, so as
wholly to exclude the light. The design and result of this contrivance is, to render it practicable
to discern objects in the water, at a very considerable depth; for the reflection of light from the water gives that element an opaque appearance,
and hides all objects from the eye, at a small distance beneath its surface. A spear-head of iron
is fastened on a pole, of about ten feet in length.

This instrument is lowered into the water ; and the fisherman, lying upon his belly, with his head under the cabin or cover, and therefore over the hole, lets down the figure of a fish, in wood, and filled with lead. Round the middle of the fish, is tied a small packthread ; and, when at the depth of ten fathom, where it is intended to be employed, it is made, by drawing the string, and by the simulta-neous pressure of the water, to move forward, after the manner of a real fish. Trout and other large fish, deceived by its resemblance, spring toward it, to seize it ; but, by a dexterous jerk of the string, it is instantly taken out of their reach. The decoy is now drawn nearer to the surface ; and the fish takes some time to renew the attack, during which the spear is raised, and held conveniently for striking. On the return of the fish, the spear is plunged into its back ; and, the spear being barbed, it is easily drawn out of the water. So completely do the rays of the light pervade the element, that in three fathom water, I have often seen the shadows of the fish, on the bottom, following them as they moved ; and this, when the ice itself was two feet in thick-ness.

By these pursuits, and others of a similar kind, we supported ourselves for two months, that is, until the twentieth of February, when we imagined the lake to be frozen, and Michilimackinac there-fore accessible ; and, the commandant wishing to go to that fort, M. Cadotte, myself, two Canadians and two Indians, agreed to accompany him. The Canadians and Indians were loaded with some parched maize, some fish, a few pieces of scorched pork, which had been saved from the fire, and a few loaves of bread, made of flour, which was also partly burnt.

We walked on snow-shoes, a mode of travelling sufficiently fatiguing to myself, but of which the commandant had had no previous experience whatever. In consequence, our progress was slow, wearisome and disastrous. On the seventh day of our march, we had only reached Point du Détour, which lies half way between the Sault and Michilimackinac; and here, to our mortification and dismay, we found the lake still open, and the ice drifting. Our provisions, too, on examination, were found to be nearly expended; and nothing remained for us to do, but to send back the Canadians and Indians, whose motions would be swift, for an additional supply.

In their absence, the commandant, M. Cadotte and myself, three persons in number, were left with about two pounds of pork and three of bread, for our subsistence during the three days, and perhaps four, which they would require, for a journey of ninety miles. Being appointed to act the part of commissary, I divided the provisions into four

parts, one for each day ; and, to our great happi‑
ness, at ten o'clock, on the fourth day, our faithful
servants returned. Early, in the morning of the
fifth, we left our encampment, and proceeded. The
weather, this day, was exceedingly cold.

We had only advanced two leagues, when the
commandant found it almost wholly impossible to
go further, his feet being blistered by the cords
of the snow‑shoes. On this account, we made
short marches, for three days ; and this loss of
time threatened us anew with famine. We were
now too far from the Sault, to send back for a
supply; and it was therefore determined that my‑
self, accompanied by one of the Canadians, should
go as speedily as possible to Michilimackinac, and
there inform the commanding officer of the situa‑
tion of those behind. Accordingly, the next morn‑
ing, at break of day, I left my fellow‑sufferers, and
at three o'clock in the afternoon had the pleasure
of entering the fort, whence a party was sent the
next morning, with provisions. This party return‑
ed on the third day, bringing with it Lieutenant
Jemette and the rest, in safety. Major Ethering‑
ton, of the sixtieth regiment, who had arrived in
the preceding autumn, now commanded at the
fort.

I remained at Michilimackinac until the 10th of
March, on which day I sat out on my return to the

Sault, taking the route of the Bay of Boutchitaouy, which the ice had now rendered practicable. From the bottom of the bay, the course lies in a direct line through the woods, a journey I performed in two days, though I was now troubled with a disorder, called the *snow-shoe evil*, proceeding from an unusual strain on the tendons of the leg, occasioned by the weight of the snow-shoe, and brings on inflammation. The remedy, prescribed in the country, is that of laying a piece of lighted touchwood on the part, and leaving it there till the flesh is burnt to the nerve ; but this experiment, though I had frequently seen it attended with success in others, I did not think proper to make upon myself.

The lands, between the Bay of Boutchitaouy and the Sault, are generally swampy, excepting so much of them as compose a ridge, or mountain, running east and west, and which is rocky, and covered with the rock or sugar maple, or sugar-wood.＊ The season, for making maple-sugar, was now at hand ; and, shortly after my arrival at the Sault, I removed, with the other inhabitants, to the place at which we were to perform the manufacture.

A certain part of the maple-woods having been chosen, and which was distant about three miles from the fort, a house, twenty feet long, and four-

＊ Acer saccharinum.

teen broad, was begun in the morning, and before
night made fit for the comfortable reception of
eight persons, and their baggage. It was open at
top, had a door at each end, and a fire-place in the
middle, running the whole length.

The next day was employed in gathering the
bark of white birch-trees, with which to make vessels to catch the wine or sap. The trees were
now cut or tapped, and spouts or ducts introduced into the wound. The bark vessels were placed
under the ducts; and, as they filled, the liquor
was taken out in buckets, and conveyed into reser-
voirs or vats of moose-skin, each vat containing a
hundred gallons. From these, we supplied the
boilers, of which we had twelve, of from twelve to
twenty gallons each, with fires constantly under
them, day and night. While the women collected
the sap, boiled it, and completed the sugar, the
men were not less busy in cutting wood, making
fires, and in hunting and fishing, in part of our
supply of food.

The earlier part of the spring is that best adapted to making maple-sugar. The sap runs only
in the day; and it will not run, unless there has
been a frost the night before. When, in the morning, there is a clear sun, and the night has left ice
of the thickness of a dollar, the greatest quantity is
produced.

On the twenty-fifth of April, our labour ended, and we returned to the fort, carrying with us, as we found by the scales, sixteen hundred weight of sugar. We had, besides, thirty-six gallons of syrup; and, during our stay in the woods, we certainly consumed three hundred weight. Though, as I have said, we hunted and fished, yet sugar was our principal food, during the whole month of April. I have known Indians to live wholly upon the same, and become fat.

On the day of our return to the fort, there arrived an English gentleman, Sir Robert Dovers, on a voyage of curiosity. I accompanied this gentleman, on his return to Michilimackinac, which we reached on the twentieth of May. My intention was to remain there, till after my clerks should have come in from the interior, and then to go back to the Sault de Sainte-Marie.

In the beginning of May, the geese and ducks made their appearance, in their progress north ward.

CHAPTER VIII.

Rumours of hostile designs, on the part of the Indians, against Michilimackinac. The Commandant wholly discredits them, and they are generally disregarded. Indians assemble, in unusual numbers, but exhibit only the most friendly behaviour. The Author is urged, by an Indian, to retire from Michilimackinac. Singular Incident. Few apprehensions are entertained within the Fort.

WHEN I reached Michilimackinac, I found several other traders, who had arrived before me, from different parts of the country, and who, in general, declared the dispositions of the Indians to be hostile to the English, and even apprehended some attack. M. Laurent Ducharme distinctly informed Major Etherington, that a plan was absolutely conceived, for destroying him, his garrison and all the English in the upper country ; but, the commandant, believing this and other reports to be without foundation, proceeding only from idle or ill-disposed persons, and of a tendency to do mischief, expressed much displeasure against M. Ducharme, and threatened to send the next person, who should bring a story of the same kind, a prisoner, to Détroit.

The garrison, at this time, consisted of ninety privates, two subalterns and the commandant; and the English merchants, at the fort, were four in number. Thus strong, few entertained anxiety concerning the Indians, who had no weapons but small arms.

Meanwhile, the Indians, from every quarter, were daily assembling, in unusual numbers, but with every appearance of friendship, frequenting the fort, and disposing of their peltries, in such a manner as to dissipate almost every one's fears. For myself, on one occasion, I took the liberty of observing to Major Etherington, that in my judgment, no confidence ought to be placed in them, and that I was informed no less than four hundred lay around the fort.

In return, the major only rallied me, on my timidity; and it is to be confessed, that if this officer neglected admonition, on his part, so did I, on mine. Shortly after my first arrival at Michilimackinac, in the preceding year, a Chipeway, named Wa'wa'tam', began to come often to my house, betraying, in his demeanour, strong marks of personal regard. After this had continued for some time, he came, on a certain day, bringing with him his whole family, and, at the same time, a large present, consisting of skins, sugar and dried meat.   Having laid these in a heap, he commenced a speech, in which he informed me, that some years before, he had observed a fast, devoting himself, according to the custom of his nation, to solitude, and to the mortification of his body, in the hope to obtain, from the Great Spirit, protection through all his days ; that on this occasion, he had dreamed of adopting an Englishman, as his son, brother and friend; that from the moment in which he first beheld me, he had recognised me as the person whom the Great Spirit had been pleased to point out to him for a brother ; that he hoped that I would not refuse his present ; and that he should forever regard me as one of his family.

I could do no otherwise than accept the present, and declare my willingness to have so good a man, as this appeared to be, for my friend and brother. I offered a present in return for that which I had received, which Wawatam accepted, and then, thanking me for the favour which he said that I had rendered him, he left me, and soon after set out on his winter's hunt.

Twelve months had now elapsed, since the occurrence of this incident, and I had almost forgotten the person of my *brother*, when, on the second day of June, Wawatam came again to my house, in a

10

temper of mind visibly melancholy and thoughtful. He told me, that he had just returned from his *wintering-ground*, and I asked after his health; but, without answering my question, he went on to say, that he was very sorry to find me returned from the Sault; that he had intended to go to that place himself, immediately after his arrival at Michilimackinac; and that he wished me to go there, along with him and his family, the next morning. To all this, he joined an inquiry, whether or not the commandant had heard bad news, adding, that, during the winter, he had himself been frequently disturbed with *the noise of evil birds;* and further suggesting, that there were numerous Indians near the fort, many of whom had never shown themselves within it.— Wawatam was about forty-five years of age, of an excellent character among his nation, and a chief.

Referring much of what I heard to the peculiarities of the Indian character, I did not pay all the attention, which they will be found to have deserved, to the entreaties and remarks of my visitor. I answered that I could not think of going to the Sault, so soon as the next morning, but would follow him there, after the arrival of my clerks. Finding himself unable to prevail with me, he withdrew, for that day; but, early the next morning, he came again, bringing with him his wife, and a present of dried meat. At this interview, after stating that he had several packs of beaver, for which he intended to deal with me, he expressed, a second time, his apprehensions, from the numerous Indians who were round the fort, and earnestly pressed me to consent to an immediate departure for the Sault.—— As a reason for this particular request, he assured me that all the Indians proposed to come in a body, that day, to the fort, to demand liquor of the commandant, and that he wished me to be gone, before they should grow intoxicated.

I had made, at the period to which I am now referring, so much progress in the language in which Wawatam addressed me, as to be able to hold an ordinary conversation in it ; but, the Indian manner of speech is so extravagantly figurative, that it is only for a very perfect master to follow and comprehend it entirely. Had I been further advanced in this respect, I think that I should have gathered so much information, from this my friendly monitor, as would have put me into possession of the design of the enemy, and enabled me to save as well others as myself ; as it was, it unfortunately happened, that I turned a deaf ear to every thing, leaving Wawatam and his wife, after long and patient, but ineffectual efforts, to depart alone, with dejected countenances, and not before they had each let fall some tears.

In the course of the same day, I observed that the Indians came in great numbers into the fort, purchasing tomahawks, (small axes, of one pound weight,) and frequently desiring to see silver arm-bands, and other valuable ornaments, of which I had a large quantity for sale.   These ornaments, however, they in no instance purchased; but, after turning them over, left them, saying, that they would call again the next day.   Their motive, as it afterward appeared, was no other than the very artful one of discovering, by requesting to see them, the particular places of their deposit, so that they might lay their hands on them in the moment of pillage with the greater certainty and dispatch.

At night, I turned in my mind the visits of Wa-watam; but, though they were calculated to excite uneasiness, nothing induced me to believe that se-rious mischief was at hand.   The next day, being the fourth of June, was the king's birth-day.

CHAPTER IX.

*The King's Birth-day being arrived, the Chipeway
and Saakies play a match at Bag'gat'iway.
Account of this game. Fort Michilimackinac
surprised and taken. General massacre of the
English. Author solicits protection from M.
Langlade—and is refused. Is concealed by a fe-
male slave. Indians drink the blood of the slain.
Author in imminent peril.*

THE morning was sultry. A Chipeway came
to tell me that his nation was going to play at *bag'-
gat'iway*, with the Sacs or Saäkies, another Indian
nation, for a high wager. He invited me to witness
the sport, adding that the commandant was to be
there, and would bet on the side of the Chipeways.
In consequence of this information, I went to the
commandant, and expostulated with him a little,
representing that the Indians might possibly have
some sinister end in view; but, the commandant
only smiled at my suspicions.

Baggatiway, called, by the Canadians, *le jeu de la crosse*, is played with a bat and ball. The bat is about four feet in length, curved, and terminating in a sort of racket. Two posts are planted in the ground, at a considerable distance from each other, as a mile, or more. Each party has its post, and the game consists in throwing the ball up to the post of the adversary. The ball, at the beginning, is placed in the middle of the course, and each party endeavours as well to throw the ball out of the direction of its own post, as into that of the adversary's.

I did not go myself to see the match which was now to be played without the fort, because, there being a canoe prepared to depart, on the following day, for Montréal, I employed myself in writing letters to my friends; and even when a fellow-trader, Mr. Tracy, happened to call upon me, saying that another canoe had just arrived from Détroit, and proposing that I should go with him to the beach, to inquire the news, it so happened that I still remained, to finish my letters; promising to follow Mr. Tracy, in the course of a few minutes. Mr. Tracy had not gone more than twenty paces from my door, when I heard an Indian war-cry, and a noise of general confusion.

Going instantly to my window, I saw a crowd of Indians, within the fort, furiously cutting down and scalping every Englishman they found.

In particular, I witnessed the fate of Lieutenant Jemette.

I had, in the room in which I was, a fowling-piece, loaded with swan-shot. This I immediately seized, and held it for a few minutes, waiting to hear the drum beat to arms. In this dreadful interval, I saw several of my countrymen fall, and more than one struggling between the knees of an Indian, who, holding him in this manner, scalped him, while yet living.

At length, disappointed in the hope of seeing resistance made to the enemy, and sensible, of course, that no effort, of my own unassisted arm, could avail against four hundred Indians, I thought only of seeking shelter. Amid the slaughter which was raging, I observed many of the Canadian inhabitants of the fort, calmly looking on, neither opposing the Indians, nor suffering injury ; and, from this circumstance, I conceived a hope of finding security in their houses.

Between the yard-door of my own house, and that of M. Langlade, my next neighbour, there was only a low fence, over which I easily climbed. At my entrance, I found the whole family at the windows, gazing at the scene of blood before them. I addressed myself immediately to M. Langlade, begging that he would put me into some place of safety, until the heat of the affair should be over; an act of charity by which he might perhaps preserve me from the general massacre; but, while I uttered my petition, M. Langlade, who had looked for a moment at me, turned again to the window, shrugging his shoulders, and intimating, that he could do nothing for me :—" *Que voudriez-vous que j'en fe-* " *rais ?*"

This was a moment for despair; but, the next, a Pani woman,* a slave of M. Langlade's, beckoned to me to follow her. She brought me to a door, which she opened, desiring me to enter, and telling me that it led to the garret, where I must go and conceal myself. I joyfully obeyed her directions; and she, having followed me up to the garret-door, locked it after me, and with great presence of mind took away the key.

This shelter obtained, if shelter I could hope to find it, I was naturally anxious to know what might still be passing without. Through an aperture, which afforded me a view of the area of the fort, I beheld, in shapes the foulest and most terrible, the ferocious triumphs of barbarian conquerors. The dead were scalped and mangled; the dying were writhing and shrieking, under the unsatiated knife and tomahawk; and, from the bodies of some,

---

* The Panies are an Indian nation of the south.

ripped open, their butchers were drinking the blood, scooped up in the hollow of joined hands, and quaffed amid shouts of rage and victory. I was shaken, not only with horror, but with fear. The sufferings which I witnessed, I seemed on the point of experiencing. No long time elapsed, before every one being destroyed, who could be found, there was a general cry, of "All is finished!" At the same instant, I heard some of the Indians enter the house in which I was.

The garret was separated from the room below, only by a layer of single boards, at once the flooring of the one and the ceiling of the other. I could therefore hear every thing that passed ; and, the Indians no sooner came in, than they inquired, whether or not any Englishman were in the house? M. Langlade replied, that " He could not say—he " did not know of any ;"—answers in which he did not exceed the truth ; for the Pani woman had not only hidden me by stealth, but kept my secret, and her own. M. Langlade was therefore, as I presume, as far from a wish to destroy me, as he was careless about saving me, when he added to these answers, that "They might examine for them. " selves, and would soon be satisfied, as to the ob- " ject of their question." Saying this, he brought them to the garret-door.

11

The state of my mind will be imagined. Arrived at the door, some delay was occasioned by the absence of the key, and a few moments were thus allowed me, in which to look around for a hiding-place. In one corner of the garret was a heap of those vessels of birch-bark, used in maple-sugar making, as I have recently described.

The door was unlocked, and opening, and the Indians ascending the stairs, before I had completely crept into a small opening, which presented itself, at one end of the heap. An instant after, four Indians entered the room, all armed with tomahawks, and all besmeared with blood, upon every part of their bodies.

The die appeared to be cast. I could scarcely breathe ; but I thought that the throbbing of my heart occasioned a noise loud enough to betray me. The Indians walked in every direction about the garret, and one of them approached me so closely that at a particular moment, had he put forth his hand, he must have touched me. Still, I remained undiscovered ; a circumstance to which the dark colour of my clothes, and the want of light, in a room which had no window, and in the corner in which I was, must have contributed. In a word, after taking several turns in the room, during which they

told M. Langlade how many they had killed, and how
many scalps they had taken, they returned down
stairs, and I, with sensations not to be expressed,
heard the door, which was the barrier between me
and my fate, locked for the second time.

There was a feather-bed on the floor ; and, on
this, exhausted as I was, by the agitation of my
mind, I threw myself down and fell asleep. In
this state I remained till the dusk of the evening,
when I was awakened by a second opening of the
door. The person, that now entered, was M.
Langlade's wife, who was much surprised at finding me, but advised me not to be uneasy, observing, that the Indians had killed most of the English,
but that she hoped I might myself escape.—A
shower of rain having begun to fall, she had come
to stop a hole in the roof. On her going away, I
begged her to send me a little water, to drink ;
which she did.

As night was now advancing, I continued to lie
on the bed, ruminating on my condition, but unable to discover a resource, from which I could
hope for life. A flight, to Détroit, had no probable chance of success. The distance, from
Michilimackinac, was four hundred miles ; I was
without provisions ; and the whole length of the
road lay through Indian countries, countries of an

enemy in arms, where the first man whom I should meet would kill me. To stay where I was, threatened nearly the same issue. As before, fatigue of mind, and not tranquillity, suspended my cares, and procured me further sleep.

CHAPTER X.

Means by which the capture of the Fort was ac-
complished. Author is betrayed—surrenders
himself to Wenniway, a Chipeway Chief—and is
spared—escapes from an Indian, who treache-
rously attempts his destruction.   Sordid inhu-
manity of M. Langlade. Author is embarked,
with other captives, for the Isles du Castor, in
Lake Michigan.

THE game of baggatiway, as from the description above will have been perceived, is necessarily
attended with much violence and noise. In the
ardour of contest, the ball, as has been suggested,
if it cannot be thrown to the goal desired, is struck in
any direction by which it can be diverted from that
designed by the adversary.   At such a moment,
therefore, nothing could be less liable to excite
premature alarm, than that the ball should be toss-
ed over the pickets of the fort, nor that having
fallen there, it should be followed, on the instant,
by all engaged in the game, as well the one party
as the other, all eager, all struggling, all shouting, all
in the unrestrained pursuit of a rude athletic exer-

cise. Nothing could be less fitted to excite premature alarm—nothing, therefore, could be more happily devised, under the circumstances, than a stratagem like this; and this was, in fact, the stratagem
which the Indians had employed, by which they
had obtained possession of the fort, and by which
they had been enabled to slaughter and subdue
its garrison, and such of its other inhabitants as
they pleased. To be still more certain of success,
they had prevailed upon as many as they could, by
a pretext the least liable to suspicion, to come voluntarily without the pickets; and particularly the
commandant and garrison themselves.

The respite which sleep afforded me, during the
night, was put an end to by the return of morning.
I was again on the rack of apprehension. At sunrise, I heard the family stirring; and, presently
after, Indian voices, informing M. Langlade that
they had not found my hapless self among the
dead, and that they supposed me to be somewhere
concealed. M. Langlade appeared, from what followed, to be, by this time, acquainted with the
place of my retreat, of which, no doubt, he had been
informed by his wife. The poor woman, as soon
as the Indians mentioned me declared to her husband, in the French tongue, that he should no
longer keep me in his house, but deliver me up to
my pursuers; giving as a reason for this measure,

that should the Indians discover his instrumentality
in my concealment, they might revenge it on her
children, and that it was better that I should die,
than they.   M. Langlade resisted, at first, this sen-
tence of his wife's ; but soon suffered her to prevail, informing the Indians that he had been told
I was in his house, that I had come there without his knowledge, and that he would put me into
their hands.   This was no sooner expressed than
he began to ascend the stairs, the Indians following
upon his heels.

I now resigned myself to the fate with which I was
menaced; and regarding every attempt at concealment as vain, I arose from the bed, and presented
myself full in view, to the Indians who were entering the room.   They were all in a state of intoxication, and entirely naked, except about the middle.
One of them, named Wenniway, whom I had previously known, and who was upward of six feet in
height, had his entire face and body covered with
charcoal and grease, only that a white spot, of two
inches in diameter, encircled either eye.   This man,
walking up to me, seized me, with one hand, by
the collar of the coat, while in the other he held a
large carving-knife, as if to plunge it into my
breast; his eyes, meanwhile, were fixed stedfast-
ly on mine.   At length, after some seconds, of the most anxious suspense, he dropped his

arm, saying, " I won't kill you !"—To this he added, that he had been frequently engaged in wars against the English, and had brought away many scalps ; that, on a certain occasion, he had lost a brother, whose name was Musinigon, and that I should be called after him.

A reprieve, upon any terms, placed me among the living, and gave me back the sustaining voice of hope ; but Wenniway ordered me down stairs, and there informing me that I was to be taken to his cabin, where, and indeed every where else, the Indians were all mad with liquor, death again was threatened, and not as possible only, but as certain. I mentioned my fears on this subject to M. Langlade, begging him to represent the danger to my master. M. Langlade, in this instance, did not withhold his compassion, and Wenniway immediately consented that I should remain where I was, until he found another opportunity to take me away.

Thus far secure, I re-ascended my garret-stairs, in order to place myself, the furthest possible, out of the reach of insult from drunken Indians ; but, I had not remained there more than an hour, when I was called to the room below, in which was an Indian, who said that I must go with him out of the fort, Wenniway having sent him to fetch

me. This man, as well as Wenniway himself, I
had seen before. In the preceding year, I had allowed him to take goods on credit, for which he
was still in my debt; and some short time previous to the surprise of the fort he had said, upon my
upbraiding him with want of honesty, that " He
" would pay me before long !"—This speech now
came fresh into my memory, and led me to suspect
that the fellow had formed a design against my
life. I communicated the suspicion to M. Langlade; but he gave for answer, that " I was not
" now my own master, and must do as I was
" ordered."

The Indian, on his part, directed, that before I
left the house, I should undress myself, declaring
that my coat and shirt would become him better
than they did me. His pleasure, in this respect,
being complied with, no other alternative was left
me than either to go out naked, or to put on the
clothes of the Indian, which he freely gave me in
exchange. His motive, for thus stripping me of
my own apparel, was no other, as I afterward learned,
than this, that it might not be stained with blood
when he should kill me.

I was now told to proceed; and my driver followed me close, until I had passed the gate of the
fort, when I turned toward the spot where I knew
the Indians to be encamped. This, however, did

12

not suit the purpose of my enemy, who seized me by the arm, and drew me violently, in the opposite direction, to the distance of fifty yards, above the fort.   Here, finding that I was approaching the bushes and sand-hills, I determined to proceed no further, but told the Indian that I believed he meant to murder me, and that if so, he might as well strike where I was, as at any greater distance.   He replied, with coolness, that my suspicions were just, and that he meant to pay me, in this manner, for my goods.   At the same time, he produced a knife, and held me in a position to receive the intended blow. Both this, and that which followed, were necessarily the affair of a moment. By some effort, too sudden and too little dependent on thought, to be explained or remembered, I was enabled to arrest his arm, and give him a sudden push, by which I turned him from me, and released myself from his grasp.   This was no sooner done, than I ran toward the fort, with all the swiftness in my power, the Indian following me, and I expecting every moment to feel his knife.—I succeeded in my flight; and, on entering the fort, I saw Wenniway, standing in the midst of the area, and to him I hastened for protection. Wenniway desired the Indian to desist; but the latter pursued me round him, making several strokes at me with his knife, and foaming at the mouth, with rage at the repeated failure of his purpose.   At length, Wenniway drew near to M. Langlade's house;

and, the door being open, I ran into it. The Indian followed me ; but, on my entering the house, he voluntarily abandoned the pursuit.

Preserved so often, and so unexpectedly, as it had now been my lot to be, I returned to my garret with a strong inclination to believe, that through the will of an overruling power, no Indian enemy could do me hurt ; but, new trials, as I believed, were at hand, when, at ten o'clock in the evening, I was roused from sleep, and once more desired to descend the stairs. Not less, however, to my satisfaction than surprise, I was summoned only to meet Major Etherington, Mr. Bostwick and Lieutenant Lesslie, who were in the room below.

These gentlemen had been taken prisoners, while looking at the game, without the fort, and immediately stripped of all their clothes. They were now sent into the fort, under the charge of Canadians, because, the Indians having resolved on getting drunk, the chiefs were apprehensive that they would be murdered, if they continued in the camp.--- Lieutenant Jemette and seventy soldiers had been killed; and but twenty Englishmen, including soldiers, were still alive. These were all within the fort, together with nearly three hundred Canadians.*

* Belonging to the canoes, &c.

These being our numbers, myself and others proposed to Major Etherington, to make an effort for regaining possession of the fort, and maintaining it against the Indians. The Jesuit missionary was consulted on the project; but he discouraged us, by his representations, not only of the merciless treatment which we must expect from the Indians, should they regain their superiority, but of the little dependence which was to be placed upon our Canadian auxiliaries. Thus, the fort and prisoners remained in the hands of the Indians, though, through the whole night, the prisoners and whites were in actual possession, and they were without the gates.

That whole night, or the greater part of it, was passed in mutual condolence; and my fellow-prisoners shared my garret. In the morning, being again called down, I found my master, Wenniway, and was desired to follow him. He led me to a small house, within the fort, where, in a narrow room, and almost dark, I found Mr. Ezekiel Solomons, an Englishman from Détroit, and a soldier, all prisoners. With these, I remained in painful suspense, as to the scene that was next to present itself, till ten o'clock, in the forenoon, when an Indian arrived, and presently marched us to the lakeside, where a canoe appeared ready for departure, and in which we found that we were to embark.

Our voyage, full of doubt as it was, would have commenced immediately, but that one of the Indians, who was to be of the party, was absent. His arrival was to be waited for ; and this occasioned a very long delay, during which we were exposed to a keen north-east wind. An old shirt was all that covered me ; I suffered much from the cold ; and, in this extremity, M. Langlade coming down to the beach, I asked him for a blanket, promising, if I lived, to pay him for it, at any price he pleased : but, the answer I received was this, that he could let me have no blanket, unless there were some one to be security for the payment. For myself, he observed, I had no longer any property in that country.—I had no more to say to M. Langlade ; but, presently seeing another Canadian, named John Cuchoise, I addressed to him a similar request, and was not refused. Naked as I was, and rigorous as was the weather, but for the blanket, I must have perished.—At noon, our party was all collected, the prisoners all embarked, and we steered for the Isles du Castor, in Lake Michigan.

CHAPTER XI.

Author and fellow-prisoners rescued, by the Otawas of L'Arbre Croche—relanded at Michilimackinac—restored to the Chipeways—lodged with other prisoners. Author sees and is recognised by Wawatam.

THE soldier, who was our companion in misfortune, was made fast to a bar of the canoe, by a rope tied round his neck, as is the manner of the Indians, in transporting their prisoners. The rest were left unconfined ; but a paddle was put into each of our hands, and we were made to use it. The Indians in the canoe were seven in number ; the prisoners four. I had left, as it will be recollected, Major Etherington, Lieutenant Lesslie and Mr. Bostwick, at M. Langlade's, and was now joined in misery with Mr. Ezekiel Solomons, the soldier, and the Englishman who had newly arrived from Détroit. This was on the sixth day of June. The fort was taken on the fourth ; I surrendered myself to Wenniway on the fifth ; and this was the third day of our distress.

We were bound, as I have said, for the Isles
du Castor, which lie in the mouth of Lake Michigan ; and we should have crossed the lake, but
that a thick fog came on, on account of which the
Indians deemed it safer to keep the shore close under their lee. We therefore approached the lands of
the Otawas, and their village of L'Arbre Croche, already mentioned as lying about twenty miles to the
westward of Michilimackinac, on the opposite side
of the tongue of land on which the fort is built.

Every half hour, the Indians gave their war-
whoops, one for every prisoner in their canoe. This
is a general custom, by the aid of which all other
Indians, within hearing, are apprized of the number
of prisoners they are carrying.

In this manner, we reached Wagoshense,* a
long point, stretching westward into the lake, and
which the Otawas make a carrying-place, to
avoid going round it. It is distant eighteen
miles from Michilimackinac. After the Indians
had made their war-whoop, as before, an Otawa
appeared upon the beach, who made signs that we
should land. In consequence, we approached.
The Otawa asked the news, and kept the Chipeways in further conversation, till we were within a
few yards of the land, and in shallow water. At

* *i. e.* Fox-point.

this moment, a hundred men rushed upon us, from among the bushes, and dragged all the prisoners out of the canoes, amid a terrifying shout.

We now believed that our last sufferings were approaching ; but, no sooner were we fairly on shore, and on our legs, than the chiefs of the party advanced, and gave each of us their hands, telling us that they were our friends, and Otawas, whom the Chipeways had insulted, by destroying the English without consulting with them on the affair. They added, that what they had done was for the purpose of saving our lives, the Chipeways having been carrying us to the Isles du Castor only to kill and devour us.

The reader's imagination is here distracted by the variety of our fortunes, and he may well paint to himself the state of mind of those who sustained them; who were the sport, or the victims, of a series of events, more like dreams than realities, more like fiction than truth ! It was not long before we were embarked again, in the canoes of the Otawas, who, the same evening, relanded us at Michilimackinac, where they marched us into the fort, in view of the Chipeways, confounded at beholding the Otawas espouse a side opposite to their own.

The Otawas, who had accompanied us in suffi-cient numbers, took possession of the fort. We, who had changed masters, but were still prisoners, were lodged in the house of the commandant, and strictly guarded.

Early the next morning, a general council was held, in which the Chipeways complained much of the conduct of the Otawas, in robbing them of their prisoners; alleging that all the Indians, the Otawas alone excepted, were at war with the English; that Pontiac had taken Détroit; that the king of France had awoke, and repossessed himself of Quebec and Montréal; and that the English were meeting destruction, not only at Michilimackinac, but in every other part of the world. From all this they inferred, that it became the Otawas to restore the prisoners, and to join in the war; and the speech was followed by large presents, being part of the plunder of the fort, and which was previously heaped in the centre of the room.—The Indians rarely make their answers till the day after they have heard the arguments offered. They did not depart from their custom on this occasion; and the council therefore adjourned.

We, the prisoners, whose fate was thus in controversy, were unacquainted, at the time, with this transaction; and therefore enjoyed a night of tolerable tranquillity, not in the least suspecting the reverse which was preparing for us. Which of the arguments of the Chipeways, or whether or not all were deemed valid by the Otawas, I cannot say; but, the council was resumed at an early hour in the morning, and, after several speeches had been made in it, the prisoners were sent for, and returned to the Chipeways.

The Otawas, who now gave us into the hands of the Chipeways, had themselves declared, that the latter designed no other than to kill us, and *make broth of us.* The Chipeways, as soon as we were restored to them, marched us to a village of their own, situate on the point which is below the fort, and put us into a lodge, already the prison of fourteen soldiers, tied two and two, with each a rope about his neck, and made fast to a pole which might be called the supporter of the building.

I was left untied; but I passed a night sleepless and full of wretchedness. My bed was the bare ground, and I was again reduced to an old shirt, as my entire apparel; the blanket which I had received, through the generosity of M. Cuchoise, having been taken from me among the Otawas, when they seized upon myself and the others, at Wagoshense. I was, besides, in want of food, having for two days ate nothing.

I confess that in the canoe, with the Chipeways, I was offered bread—but, bread, with what accompaniment!—They had a loaf, which they cut with the same knives that they had employed in the massacre—knives still covered with blood. The blood, they moistened with spittle, and rubbing it on the bread, offered this for food to their prisoners, telling them to eat the blood of their countrymen.

Such was my situation, on the morning of the seventh of June, in the year one thousand seven hundred and sixty-three ; but, a few hours produced an event which gave still a new colour to my lot.

Toward noon, when the great war-chief, in company with Wenniway, was seated at the opposite end of the lodge, my friend and brother, Wawatam, suddenly came in. During the four days preceding, I had often wondered what had become of him. In passing by, he gave me his hand, but went immediately toward the great chief, by the side of whom and Wenniway, he sat himself down. The most uninterrupted silence prevailed ; each smoked his pipe ; and this done, Wawatam arose, and left the lodge, saying, to me, as he passed, " Take courage !"

CHAPTER XII.

AN hour elapsed, during which several chiefs entered, and preparations appeared to be making for a council. At length, Wawatam re-entered the lodge, followed by his wife, and both loaded with merchandize, which they carried up to the chiefs, and laid in a heap before them. Some moments of silence followed, at the end of which Wawatam pronounced a speech, every word of which, to me, was of extraordinary interest :

" Friends and relations," he began, " what is it " that I shall say ? You know what I feel. You " all have friends and brothers and children, whom " as yourselves you love ; and you—what would

" you experience, did you, like me, behold your
" dearest friend—your brother—in the condition of
" a slave ; a slave, exposed every moment to in-
" sult, and to menaces of death ? This case, as you
" all know, is mine. See there (*pointing to myself*)
" my friend and brother among slaves—himself a
" slave !

" You all well know, that long before the war
" began, I adopted him as my brother. From that
" moment, he became one of my family, so that
" no change of circumstances could break the cord
" which fastened us together.

" He is my brother ; and, because I am your
" relation, he is therefore your relation too :—and
" how, being your relation, can he be your slave ?

" On the day, on which the war began, you were
" fearful, lest, on this very account, I should reveal
" your secret. You requested, therefore, that I
" would leave the fort, and even cross the lake. I
" did so ; but I did it with reluctance. I did it
" with reluctance, notwithstanding that you, Me-
" nehwehna, who had the command in this enter-
" prise, gave me your promise that you would pro-
" tect my friend, delivering him from all danger,
" and giving him safely to me.

" The performance of this promise, I now claim.
" I come not with empty hands to ask it.   You,
" Menehwehna, best know, whether or not, as it
" respects yourself, you have kept your word , but
" I bring these goods, to buy off every claim which
" any man among you all may have on my bro-
" ther, as his prisoner."

Wawatam having ceased, the pipes were again
filled ; and, after they were finished, a further period of silence followed.   At the end of this, Menehwehna arose, and gave his reply :

" My relation and brother," said he, " what you
" have spoken is the truth.   We were acquainted
" with the friendship which subsisted between
" yourself and the Englishman, in whose behalf
" you have now addressed us.   We knew the
" danger of having our secret discovered, and
" the consequences which must follow ; and you
" say truly, that we requested you to leave the
" fort.   This we did, out of regard for you and
" your family ; for, if a discovery of our design
" had been made, you would have been blamed,
" whether guilty or not ; and you would thus have
" been involved in difficulties from which you
" could not have extricated yourself.

" It is also true, that I promised you to take care
" of your friend ; and this promise I performed,

" by desiring my son, at the moment of assault, to
" seek him out, and bring him to my lodge.   He
" went accordingly, but could not find him.   The
" day after, I sent him to Langlade's, when he was
" informed that your friend was safe ; and had
" it not been that the Indians were then drink-
" ing the rum which had been found in the fort, he
" would have brought him home with him, accord-
" ing to my orders.

    " I am very glad to find that your friend has
" escaped.   We accept your present ; and you
" may take him home with you."

    Wawatam thanked the assembled chiefs, and
taking me by the hand, led me to his lodge, which
was at the distance of a few yards only from
the prison-lodge.   My entrance appeared to give
joy to the whole family ; food was immediately prepared for me ; and I now ate the first hearty meal
which I had made since my capture.   I found myself one of the family ; and but that I had still my
fears, as to the other Indians, I felt as happy as the
situation could allow.

    In the course of the next morning, I was alarm-
ed by a noise in the prison-lodge ; and looking
through the openings of the lodge in which I was,
I saw seven dead bodies of white men dragged
forth.   Upon my inquiry into the occasion, I was

informed, that a certain chief, called, by the Canadians, Le Grand Sable, had not long before arrived from his winter's hunt; and that he, having been absent when the war begun, and being now desirous of manifesting to the Indians at large, his hearty concurrence in what they had done, had gone into the prison-lodge, and there, with his knife, put the seven men, whose bodies I had seen, to death.

Shortly after, two of the Indians took one of the dead bodies, which they chose as being the fattest, cut off the head, and divided the whole into five parts, one of which was put into each of five kettles, hung over as many fires, kindled for this purpose, at the door of the prison-lodge. Soon after things were so far prepared, a message came to our lodge, with an invitation to Wawatam, to assist at the feast.

An invitation to a feast is given by him who is the master of it. Small cuttings of cedar-wood, of about four inches in length, supply the place of cards; and the bearer, by word of mouth, states the particulars.

Wawatam obeyed the summons, taking with him, as is usual, to the place of entertainment, his dish and spoon.

After an absence of about half an hour, he returned, bringing in his dish a human hand, and

a large piece of flesh.   He did not appear to relish
the repast, but told me, that it was then, and always
had been the custom, among all the Indian nations,
when returning from war, or on overcoming their
enemies, to make a war-feast, from among the
slain.   This, he said, inspired the warrior with
courage in attack, and bred him to meet death with
fearlessness.

In the evening of the same day, a large canoe,
such as those which came from Montréal, was
seen advancing to the fort.   It was full of men,
and I distinguished several passengers.   The Indian cry was made in the village ; a general muster
ordered ; and, to the number of two hundred, they
marched up to the fort, where the canoe was expected to land.   The canoe, suspecting nothing,
came boldly to the fort, where the passengers, as
being English traders, were seized, dragged through
the water, beat, reviled, marched to the prison-.
lodge, and there stripped of their clothes, and confined.

Of the English traders that fell into the hands of
the Indians, at the capture of the fort, Mr. Tracy
was the only one who lost his life.   Mr. Ezekiel
Solomons and Mr. Henry Bostwick were taken
by the Otawas, and, after the peace, carried down
to Montréal, and there ransomed. Of ninety troops,

14

about seventy were killed; the rest, together with those of the posts in the Bay des Puants, and at the river Saint-Joseph, were also kept in safety by the Otawas, till the peace, and then either freely restored, or ransomed at Montréal. The Otawas never overcame their disgust, at the neglect with which they had been treated, in the beginning of the war, by those who afterward desired their assistance as allies.

CHAPTER XIII.

Indians entertain apprehensions of the English—re-
solve to retire to the Island of Michilimackinac.
A gale of wind—and Indians sacrifice a Dog.
Women lament at the burial-place of Relations.
Land on the Island. Number of Warriors.
Author hid by Wawatam in a cave—makes a
discovery there. Indian explanations. Indian
sacrifices.

IN the morning of the ninth of June, a general
council was held, at which it was agreed to remove
to the island of Michilimackinac, as a more defen-
sible situation, in the event of an attack by the English.   The Indians had begun to entertain apprehensions of want of strength.   No news had reached them from the Potawatamies, in the Bay des
Puants ; and they were uncertain whether or not
the Monomins* would join them.   They even

* Manomines, or Malomines.   In the first syllable, the
substitution of *l* for *n,* and *n* for *l,* marks one of the differen-
ces in the Chipeway and Algonquin dialects.

In the mouth of an Algonquin, it is *Michilimackinac ;*
in that of a Chipeway, *Michinimackinac.*

feared that the Sioux would take the English side.

This resolution fixed, they prepared for a speedy retreat. At noon, the camp was broken up, and we embarked, taking with us the prisoners that were still undisposed of. On our passage, we encountered a gale of wind, and there were some appearances of danger. To avert it, a dog, of which the legs were previously tied together, was thrown into the lake ; an offering designed to soothe the angry passions of some offended Ma'ni'to'.

As we approached the island, two women, in the canoe in which I was, began to utter melancholy and hideous cries. Precarious as my condition still remained, I experienced some sensations of alarm, from these dismal sounds, of which I could not then discover the occasion. Subsequently, I learned, that it is customary for the women, on passing near the burial-places of relations, never to omit the practice of which I was now a witness, and by which they intend to denote their grief.

By the approach of evening, we reached the island in safety, and the women were not long in erecting our cabins. In the morning, there was a muster of the Indians, at which there were found three hundred and fifty fighting-men.

In the course of the day, there arrived a canoe from Détroit, with ambassadors, who endeavoured to prevail on the Indians to repair thither, to the assistance of Pontiac; but fear was now the prevailing passion. A guard was kept during the day, and a watch by night, and alarms were very frequently spread. Had an enemy appeared, all the prisoners would have been put to death; and I suspected, that as an Englishman, I should share their fate.

Several days had now passed, when, one morning, a continued alarm prevailed, and I saw the Indians running, in a confused manner, toward the beach. In a short time, I learned that two large canoes, from Montréal, were in sight.

All the Indian canoes were immediately manned, and those from Montréal were surrounded and seized, as they turned a point, behind which the flotilla had been concealed. The goods were consigned to a Mr. Levy, and would have been saved, if the canoe-men had called them French property; but they were terrified, and disguised nothing.

In the canoes was a large proportion of liquor, a dangerous acquisition, and which threatened disturbance among the Indians, even to the loss of their dearest friends. Wawatam, always watchful of my safety, no sooner heard the noise of drunkenness, which, in the evening, did not fail to begin, than he represented to me the danger of remaining in the village, and owned that he could not himself resist the temptation of joining his comrades in the debauch. That I might escape all mischief, he therefore requested that I would accompany him to the mountain, where I was to remain hidden, till the liquor should be drank.

We ascended the mountain accordingly. It is this mountain which constitutes that high land, in the middle of the island, of which I have spoken before, as of a figure considered as resembling a *turtle*, and therefore called *michilimackinac*. It is thickly covered with wood, and very rocky toward the top. After walking more than half a mile, we came to a large rock, at the base of which was an opening, dark within, and appearing to be the entrance of a cave.

Here, Wawatam recommended that I should take up my lodging, and by all means remain till he returned.

On going into the cave, of which the entrance was nearly ten feet wide, I found the further end to be rounded in its shape, like that of an oven, but with a further aperture, too small, however, to be explored.

After thus looking around me, I broke small branches from the trees, and spread them for a bed; then wrapped myself in my blanket, and slept till day-break.

On awaking, I felt myself incommoded by some object, upon which I lay; and, removing it, found it to be a bone. This I supposed to be that of a deer, or some other animal, and what might very naturally be looked for, in the place in which I was; but, when day-light visited my chamber, I discovered, with some feelings of horror, that I was lying on nothing less than a heap of human bones and skulls, which covered all the floor!

The day passed without the return of Wawatam, and without food. As night approached, I found myself unable to meet its darkness in the charnel-house, which, nevertheless, I had viewed free from uneasiness during the day. I chose, therefore, an adjacent bush for this night's lodging, and slept under it as before; but, in the morning, I awoke hungry and dispirited, and almost envying the dry bones, to the view of which I returned. At length, the sound of a foot reached me, and my Indian friend appeared, making many apologies for his long absence, the cause of which was an unfortunate excess in the enjoyment of his liquor.

This point being explained, I mentioned the extraordinary sight that had presented itself, in the cave to which he had commended my slumbers. He had never heard of its existence before ; and, upon examining the cave together, we saw reason to believe that it had been anciently filled with human bodies.

On returning to the lodge, I experienced a cordial reception from the family, which consisted of the wife of my friend, his two sons, of whom the eldest was married, and whose wife, and a daughter, of thirteen years of age, completed the list.

Wawatam related to the other Indians the adventure of the bones. All of them expressed surprise at hearing it, and declared that they had never been aware of the contents of this cave before. After visiting it, which they immediately did, almost every one offered a different opinion, as to its history.

Some advanced, that at a period when the waters overflowed the land, (an event which makes a distinguished figure in the history of their world,) the inhabitants of this island had fled into the cave, and been there drowned; others, that those same inhabitants, when the Hurons made war upon them, (as tradition says they did,) hid themselves in the cave, and being discovered, were there massacred. For myself, I am disposed to believe, that this cave was an ancient receptacle of the bones of prisoners, sacrificed and devoured at war-feasts. I have always observed, that the Indians pay particular attention to the bones of sacrifices, preserving them unbroken, and depositing them in some place kept exclusively for that purpose.

CHAPTER XIV.

Care of Menehwehna for the Author's preserva-
tion. Author assumes the Indian Costume—in
what that Costume consists. Provisions scarce.
Indian resignation. Family remove to the Bay
of Boutchitaouy. Indian Medicines. Pretended
Sorceries. Cures of Flesh-wounds.

A FEW days after the occurrence of the incidents recorded in the preceding chapter, Menehwehna, whom I now found to be the great chief
of the village of Michilimackinac, came to the
lodge of my friend ; and when the usual ceremony
of smoking was finished, he observed that Indians were now daily arriving from Détroit, some
of whom had lost relations or friends in the war,
and who would certainly retaliate on any Englishman they found ; upon which account, his errand was to advise that I should be dressed like
an Indian, an expedient whence I might hope to
escape all future insult.

I could not but consent to the proposal, and the
chief was so kind as to assist my friend and his fa-

mily in effecting that very day the desired metamor-
phosis. My hair was cut off, and my head shaved,
with the exception of a spot on the crown, of about
twice the diameter of a crown-piece. My face was
painted with three or four different colours ; some
parts of it red, and others black. A shirt was provided for me, painted with vermilion, mixed with
grease. A large collar of wampum was put round
my neck, and another suspended on my breast.
Both my arms were decorated with large bands of
silver above the elbow, besides several smaller ones
on the wrists; and my legs were covered with *mitas-
ses*, a kind of hose, made, as is the favourite fashion,
of scarlet cloth. Over all, I was to wear a scarlet
blanket or mantle, and on my head a large bunch
of feathers. I parted, not without some regret,
with the long hair which was natural to it, and
which I fancied to be ornamental ; but the ladies of
the family, and of the village in general, appeared
to think my person improved, and now condescend-
ed to call me handsome, even among Indians.

Protected, in a great measure, by this disguise,
I felt myself more at liberty than before ; and the
season being arrived in which my clerks, from the
interior, were to be expected, and some part of my
property, as I had a right to hope, recovered, I
begged the favour of Wawatam, that he would
enable me to pay a short visit to Michilimackinac.
He did not fail to comply, and I succeeded in find-

ing my clerks ; but, either through the disturbed state of the country, as they represented to be the case, or through their misconduct, as I had reason to think, I obtained nothing ;—and nothing, or almost nothing, I now began to think, would be all that I should need, during the rest of my life.   To fish and to hunt, to collect a few skins, and ex-change them for necessaries, was all that I seemed destined to do, and to acquire, for the future.

I returned to the Indian village, where at this time much scarcity of food prevailed.   We were often for twenty-four hours without eating ; and when in the morning we had no victuals for the day before us, the custom was to black our faces with grease and charcoal, and exhibit, through re-signation, a temper as cheerful as if in the midst of plenty.

A repetition of the evil, however, soon induced us to leave the island, in search of food ; and ac-cordingly we departed for the Bay of Boutchitaouy, distant eight leagues, and where we found plenty of wild-fowl and fish.

While in the bay, my guardian's daughter-in-law was taken in labour, of her first child.   She was immediately removed out of the common lodge ; and a small one, for her separate accommodation, was begun and finished by the women in less than half an hour.

The next morning, we heard that she was very ill, and the family began to be much alarmed on her account; the more so, no doubt, because cases of difficult labour are very rare among Indian women. In this distress, Wawatam requested me to accompany him into the woods; and on our way informed me, that if he could find a snake, he should soon secure relief to his daughter-in-law.

On reaching some wet ground, we speedily obtained the object of our search, in a small snake, of the kind called the garter-snake. Wawatam seized it by the neck; and, holding it fast, while it coiled itself round his arm, he cut off its head, catching the blood in a cup that he had brought with him. This done, he threw away the snake, and carried home the blood, which he mixed with a quantity of water. Of this mixture, he administered first one table-spoonful, and shortly after a second. Within an hour, the patient was safely delivered of a fine child; and Wawatam subsequently declared, that the remedy, to which he had resorted, was one that never failed.

On the next day, we left the Bay of Boutchitaouy; and the young mother, in high spirits, assisted in loading the canoe, barefooted, and knee-deep in the water.

The medical information, the diseases and the remedies of the Indians, often engaged my curiosity, during the period through which I was familiar with these nations; and I shall take this occasion to introduce a few particulars, connected with their history.

The Indians are in general free from disorders; and an instance of their being subject to dropsy, gout, or stone, never came within my knowledge. Inflammations of the lungs are among their most ordinary complaints, and rheumatism still more so, especially with the aged. Their mode of life, in which they are so much exposed to the wet and cold, sleeping on the ground, and inhaling the night air, sufficiently accounts for their liability to these diseases. The remedies, on which they most rely, are emetics, cathartics and the lancet; but especially the last. Bleeding is so favourite an operation among the women, that they never lose an occasion of enjoying it, whether sick or well. I have sometimes bled a dozen women in a morning, as they sat in a row, along a fallen tree, beginning with the first—opening the vein—then proceeding to the second—and so on, having three or four individuals bleeding at the same time.

In most villages, and particularly in those of the Chipeways, this service was required of me ; and no persuasion of mine could ever induce a woman to dispense with it.

In all parts of the country, and among all the nations that I have seen, particular individuals arrogate to themselves the art of healing, but principally by means of pretended sorcery ; and operations of this sort are always paid for by a present, made before they are begun. Indeed, whatever, as an impostor, may be the demerits of the operator, his reward may generally be said to be fairly earned, by dint of corporal labour.

I was once present at a performance of this kind, in which the patient was a female child of about twelve years of age. Several of the elder chiefs were invited to the scene ; and the same compliment was paid to myself, on account of the medical skill for which it was pleased to give me credit.

The physician (so to call him) seated himself on the ground ; and before him, on a new stroud blanket, was placed a bason of water, in which were three bones, the larger ones, as it appeared to me, of a swan's wing. In his hand, he had his *shishiquoi*, or rattle, with which he beat time to his *medicine-song*. The sick child lay on a blanket, near the physician. She appeared to have much fever, and a severe oppression of the lungs, breathing with difficulty, and betraying symptoms of the last stage of consumption.

After singing for some time, the physician took one of the bones out of the basón : the bone was hollow ; and one end being applied to the breast of the patient, he put the other into his mouth, in order to remove the disorder by suction. Having persevered in this as long as he thought proper, he suddenly seemed to force the bone into his mouth, and swallow it. He now acted the part of one suffering severe pain ; but, presently finding relief, he made a long speech, and after this, returned to singing, and to the accompaniment of his rattle. With the latter, during his song, he struck his head, breast, sides and back ; at the same time straining, as if to vomit forth the bone.

Relinquishing this attempt, he applied himself to suction a second time, and with the second of the three bones ; and this also he soon seemed to swallow.

Upon its disappearance, he began to distort himself in the most frightful manner, using every gesture which could convey the idea of pain : at length, he succeeded, or pretended to succeed, in throwing up one of the bones. This was handed about to the spectators, and strictly examined; but nothing remarkable could be discovered. Upon this, he went back to his song and rattle; and after some time threw up the second of the two bones. In the groove of this, the physician, upon examination, found, and displayed to all present, a small white substance, resembling a piece of the quill of a feather. It was passed round the company, from one to the other; and declared, by the physician, to be the thing causing the disorder of his patient.

The multitude believe that these physicians, whom the French call *jongleurs*, or jugglers, can inflict as well as remove disorders. They believe, that by drawing the figure of any person in sand or ashes, or on clay, or by considering any object as the figure of a person, and then pricking it with a sharp stick, or other substance, or doing in any other manner, that which done to a living body, would cause pain or injury, the individual represented, or supposed to be represented, will suffer accordingly. On the other hand, the mischief being done, another physician, of equal pretensions, can by suction remove it.—Unfortunately, however, the operations which I have described were not successful, in the instance referred to ; for, on the day after they had taken place, the girl died.

16

With regard to flesh-wounds, the Indians certainly effect astonishing cures. Here, as above, much that is fantastic occurs ; but the success of their practice evinces something solid.

At the Sault de Sainte-Marie, I knew a man, who, in the result of a quarrel, received the stroke of an axe in his side. The blow was so violent, and the axe driven so deep, that the wretch who held it could not withdraw it, but left it in the wound, and fled. Shortly after, the man was found, and brought into the fort, where several other Indians came to his assistance. Among these, one, who was a physician, immediately withdrew, in order to fetch his *penegusan*, or medicine-bag, with which he soon returned. The eyes of the sufferer were fixed, his teeth closed, and his case apparently desperate.

The physician took from his bag a small portion of a very white substance, resembling that of a bone ; this he scraped into a little water, and forcing open the jaws of the patient with a stick, he poured the mixture down his throat. What followed was, that in a very short space of time, the wounded man moved his eyes ; and beginning to vomit, threw up a small lump of clotted blood.

The physician now, and not before, examined the wound, from which I could see the breath escape, and from which a part of the omentum de-

pended.   This, the physician did not set about to
restore to its place; but, cutting it away, minced it
into small pieces, and made his patient swallow it.

The man was then carried to his lodge, where I
visited him daily. By the sixth day, he was able to
walk about ; and within a month he grew quite
well, except that he was troubled with a cough.
Twenty years after his misfortune, he was still
alive.

Another man, being on his wintering-ground,
and from home, hunting beaver, was crossing a
lake, covered with smooth ice, with two beavers
on his back, when his foot slipped, and he fell.
At his side, in his belt, was his axe, the blade of
which came upon the joint of his wrist ; and, the
weight of his body coming upon the blade, his hand
was completely separated from his arm, with the
exception of a small piece of the skin.   He had to
walk three miles to his lodge, which was thus far
away.   The skin, which alone retained his hand
to his arm, he cut through, with the same axe which
had done the rest ; and fortunately having on a
shirt, he took it off, tore it up, and made a strong
ligature above the wrist, so as in some measure to
avoid the loss of blood.   On reaching his lodge, he
cured the wound himself, by the mere use of sim-
ples.   I was a witness to its perfect healing.

I have said, that these physicians, jugglers, or practitioners of pretended sorcery, are supposed to be capable of inflicting diseases; and I may add, that they are sometimes themselves sufferers on this account. In one instance, I saw one of them killed, by a man who charged him with having brought his brother to death, by malefic arts. The accuser, in his rage, thrust his knife into the belly of the accused, and ripped it open. The latter caught his bowels in his arms, and thus walked toward his lodge, gathering them up from time to time, as they escaped his hold. His lodge was at no considerable distance, and he reached it alive, and died in it.

CHAPTER XV.

Encamp on the Island of Saint-Martin. Sturgeon
fishery. Remove to Wintering-ground, in Lake
Michigan. Geographical Remarks. Beaver-
hunting. Indian Devotion. Beaver. Racoon-
hunting.

OUR next encampment was on the island of
Saint-Martin, off Cape Saint-Ignace, so called from
the Jesuit mission of Saint Ignatius to the Hurons, formerly established there. Our object was
to fish for sturgeon, which we did with great success ; and here, in the enjoyment of a plentiful and
excellent supply of food, we remained until the
twentieth day of August. At this time, the autumn
being at hand, and a sure prospect of increased
security from hostile Indians afforded, Wawatam
proposed going to his intended wintering-ground.
The removal was a subject of the greatest joy to
myself, on account of the frequent insults, to which
I had still to submit, from the Indians of our band
or village; and to escape from which I would freely
have gone almost any where. At our wintering-
ground, we were to be alone ; for the Indian families, in the countries of which I write, separate in

the winter season, for the convenience, as well of subsistence as of the chase, and re-associate in the spring and summer.

In preparation, our first business was to sail for Michilimackinac, where, being arrived, we procured from a Canadian trader, on credit, some trifling articles, together with ammunition, and two bushels of maize. This done, we steered directly for Lake Michigan. At L'Arbre Croche we stopped one day, on a visit to the Otawas, where all the people, and particularly O'ki'no'chu'ma'ki', the chief, the same who took me from the Chipeways, behaved with great civility and kindness. The chief presented me with a bag of maize. It is the Otawas, it will be remembered, who raise this grain, for the market of Michilimackinac.

Leaving L'Arbre Croche, we proceeded direct to the mouth of the river Aux Sables, on the south side of the lake, and distant about a hundred and fifty miles from Fort Michilimackinac. On our voyage, we passed several deep bays and rivers, and I found the banks of the lake to consist in mere sands, without any appearance of verdure; the sand drifting from one hill to another, like snow in winter. Hence, all the rivers, which here entered the lake, are as much entitled to the epithet of *sandy*, as that to which we were bound. They are also distinguished by another particularity,

always observable in similar situations. The current of the stream being met, when the wind is contrary, by the waves of the lake, it is driven back,
and the sands of the shore are at the same time
washed into its mouth. In consequence, the river
is able to force a passage into the lake, broad only
in proportion to its utmost strength; while it hollows for itself, behind the sand-banks, a bason of
one, two, or three miles across. In these rivers we
killed many wild-fowl and beaver.

To kill beaver, we used to go several miles up
the rivers, before the approach of night, and after
the dusk came on, suffer the canoe to drift gently
down the current, without noise. The beaver, in
this part of the evening, come abroad to procure
food, or materials for repairing their habitations;
and as they are not alarmed by the canoe, they often
pass it within gun-shot.

While we thus hunted along our way, I enjoyed
a personal freedom of which I had been long de
prived, and became as expert in the Indian pur
suits, as the Indians themselves.

On entering the river Aux Sables, Wawatam
took a dog, tied its feet together, and threw it
into the stream, uttering, at the same time, a long
prayer, which he addressed to the Great Spirit,
supplicating his blessing on the chase, and his aid

in the support of the family, through the dangers of a long winter.—Our lodge was fifteen miles above the mouth of the stream. The principal animals, which the country afforded, were the stag or red-deer, the common American deer, the bear, ra-coon, beaver and marten.

The beaver feeds in preference on young wood of the birch, aspen, and poplar-tree;* but, in defect of these, on any other tree, those of the pine and fir kinds excepted. These latter it employs only for building its dams and houses. In wide mea-dows, where no wood is to be found, it resorts, for all its purposes, to the roots of the rush and water-lily. It consumes great quantities of food, whether of roots or wood; and hence often reduces itself to the necessity of removing into a new quarter. Its house has an arched dome-like roof, of an elip-tical figure, and rises from three to four feet above the surface of the water. It is always entirely sur-rounded by water; but, in the banks adjacent, the animal provides holes or *washes*, of which the en-trance is below the surface, and to which it retreats on the first alarm.

The female beaver usually produces two young at a time, but not unfrequently more. During the

---

*Populus nigra, called, by the Canadians, *liard*.

first year, the young remain with their parents. In the second, they occupy an adjoining apartment, and assist in building, and in procuring food. At two years old, they part, and build houses of their own ; but often rove about for a considerable time, before they fix upon a spot. There are beavers, called, by the Indians, *old bachelors*, who live by themselves, build no houses, and work at no dams, but shelter themselves in holes. The usual method of taking these is by traps, formed of iron, or logs, and baited with branches of poplar.

According to the Indians, the beaver is much given to jealousy. If a strange male approaches the cabin, a battle immediately ensues. Of this, the female remains an unconcerned spectator, care-less to which party the law of conquest may assign her. Among the beaver which we killed, those who were with me pretended to show demonstra-tions of this fact ; some of the skins of the males, and almost all of the older ones, bearing marks of violence, while none were ever to be seen on the skins of the females.

The Indians add, that the male is as constant as he is jealous, never attaching himself to more than one female ; while the female, on her side, is always fond of strangers.

The most common way of taking the beaver is
that of breaking up its house, which is done with
trenching-tools, during the winter, when the ice is
strong enough to allow of approaching them ; and
when, also, the fur is in its most valuable state.

Breaking up the house, however, is only a pre-
paratory step.   During this operation, the family
make their escape to one or more of their *washes*.
These are to be discovered, by striking the ice
along the bank, and where the holes are, a hollow
sound is returned. After discovering and search-
ing many of these in vain, we often found the whole
family together, in the same wash.   I was taught
occasionally to distinguish a full wash from an empty
one, by the motion of the water above its entrance,
occasioned by the breathing of the animals concealed in it.   From the washes, they must be taken
out with the hands ; and in doing this, the hunter
sometimes receives severe wounds from their teeth.
While a hunter, I thought, with the Indians, that
the beaver-flesh was very good ; but after that
of the ox was again within my reach, I could
not relish it.   The tail is accounted a luxurious
morsel.

Beavers, say the Indians, were formerly a people endowed with speech, not less than with the
other noble faculties they possess ; but, the Great

Spirit has taken this away from them, lest they should grow superior in understanding to mankind.

The racoon was another object of our chase. It was my practice to go out in the evening, with dogs, accompanied by the youngest son of my guardian, to hunt this animal. The racoon never leaves its hiding-place till after sun-set.

As soon as a dog falls on a fresh track of the racoon, he gives notice by a cry, and immediately pursues. His barking enables the hunter to follow. The racoon, which travels slowly, and is soon overtaken, makes for a tree, on which he remains till shot.

After the falling of the snow, nothing more is necessary, for taking the racoon, than to follow the track of his feet. In this season, he seldom leaves his habitation ; and he never lays up any food. I have found six at a time, in the hollow of one tree, lying upon each other, and nearly in a torpid state. In more than one instance, I have ascertained that they have lived six weeks without food. The mouse is their principal prey.

Racoon-hunting was my more particular and daily employ. I usually went out at the first dawn of day, and seldom returned till sun-set, or till I had laden myself with as many animals as I could carry. By degrees, I became familiarized with this kind of life ; and had it not been for the idea of which I could not divest my mind, that I was living among savages, and for the whispers of a lingering hope, that I should one day be released from it—or if I could have forgotten that I had ever been other-wise than as I then was—I could have enjoyed as much happiness in this, as in any other situation.

CHAPTER XVI.

Feast of the Manes of Relations and Friends. Pro-
duct of Chase. Indian Family set out on a Hunt-
ing Excursion. Indian travelling by Land.
Author loses his Way.

ONE evening, on my return from hunting, I
found the fire put out, and the opening, in the top
of the lodge, covered over with skins; by this
means excluding, as much as possible, external
light. I further observed, that the ashes were
removed from the fire-place, and that dry sand was
spread where they had been. Soon after, a fire
was made without side the cabin, in the open air,
and a kettle hung over it to boil.

I now supposed that a feast was in preparation.
I supposed so, only; for it would have been inde-
corous to inquire into the meaning of what I saw.
No person, among the Indians themselves, would
use this freedom. Good-breeding requires that the
spectator should patiently wait the result.

As soon as the darkness of night had arrived, the family, including myself, were invited into the lodge. I was now requested not to speak, as a feast was about to be given to the dead, whose spirits delight in uninterrupted silence.

As we entered, each was presented with his wooden-dish and spoon, after receiving which we seated ourselves. The door was next shut, and we remained in perfect darkness.

The master of the family was the master of the feast. Still in the dark, he asked every one, by turn, for his dish, and put into each two boiled ears of maize. The whole being served, he began to speak. In his discourse, which lasted half an hour, he called upon the manes of his deceased relations and friends, beseeching them to be present, to assist him in the chase, and to partake of the food which he had prepared for them. When he had ended, we proceeded to eat our maize, which we did without other noise than what was occasioned by our teeth. The maize was not half boiled, and it took me an hour to consume my share. I was requested not to break the spikes,* as this would be displeasing to the departed spirits of their friends.

---

* The grains of maize, called also Indian corn, grow in compact cells, round a spike.

When all was eaten, Wawatam made another speech, with which the ceremony ended. A new fire was kindled, with fresh sparks, from flint and steel; and the pipes being smoked, the spikes were carefully buried, in a hole made in the ground for that purpose, within the lodge. This done, the whole family began a dance, Wawatam singing, and beating a drum. The dance continued the greater part of the night, to the great pleasure of the lodge.—The night of the feast was that of the first day of November.

On the twentieth of December, we took an account of the produce of our hunt, and found that we had a hundred beaver-skins, as many racoons, and a large quantity of dried venison; all which was secured from the wolves, by being placed upon a scaffold.

A hunting-excursion, into the interior of the country, was resolved on; and, early the next morning, the bundles were made up by the women, for each person to carry. I remarked, that the bundle given to me was the lightest, and those carried by the women, the largest and heaviest of the whole.

On the first day of our march, we advanced about twenty miles, and then encamped. Being somewhat fatigued, I could not hunt; but Wawatam killed a stag, not far from our encampment. The next morning, we moved our lodge to the carcass. At this station, we remained two days, employed in drying the meat. The method was to cut it into slices, of the thickness of a steak, and then hang it over the fire, in the smoke. On the third day, we removed, and marched till two o'clock in the after- noon.

While the women were busy in erecting and preparing the lodges, I took my gun, and strolled away, telling Wawatam that I intended to look out for some fresh meat, for supper. He answered, that he would do the same ; and, on this, we both left the encampment, in different directions.

The sun being visible, I entertained no fear of losing my way ; but, in following several tracks of animals, in momentary expectation of falling in with the game, I proceeded to a considerable distance, and it was not till near sun-set that I thought of re- turning. The sky, too, had become overcast, and I was therefore left without the sun for my guide. In this situation, I walked as fast as I could, always supposing myself to be approaching our encamp- ment, till at length it became so dark that I ran against the trees.

I became convinced that I was lost ; and I was alarmed by the reflection, that I was in a country entirely strange to me, and in danger from strange Indians. With the flint of my gun, I made a fire, and then laid me down to sleep. In the night, it rained hard. I awoke, cold and wet ; and as soon as light appeared, I recommenced my journey, sometimes walking and sometimes running, un-knowing where to go, bewildered, and like a mad-man.

Toward evening, I reached the border of a large lake, of which I could scarcely discern the opposite shore. I had never heard of a lake in this part of the country, and therefore felt myself removed fur-ther than ever from the object of my pursuit. To tread back my steps appeared to be the most likely means of delivering myself; and I accordingly de-termined to turn my face directly from the lake, and keep this direction as nearly as I could.

A heavy snow began to descend, and night soon afterward came on. On this, I stopped and made a fire ; and stripping a tree of its sheet of bark, lay down under it, to shelter me from the snow. All night, at small distances, the wolves howled around; and, to me, seemed to be acquainted with my mis-fortune.

Amid thoughts the most distracted, I was able, at length, to fall asleep ; but it was not long before I awoke, refreshed, and wondering at the terror to which I had yielded myself. That I could really have wanted the means of recovering my way, appeared to me almost incredible ; and the recollection of it like a dream, or as a circumstance which must have proceeded from the loss of my senses. Had this not happened, I could never, as I now thought, have suffered so long, without calling to mind the lessons which I had received from my Indian friend, for the very purpose of being useful to me, in difficulties of this kind. These were, that generally speaking, the tops of pine-trees lean toward the rising of the sun ; that moss grows toward the roots of trees, on the side which faces the north; and that the limbs of trees are most numerous, and largest, on that which faces the south.

Determined to direct my feet by these marks, and persuaded that I should thus, sooner or later, reach Lake Michigan, which I reckoned to be distant about sixty miles, I began my march at break of day. I had not taken, nor wished to take, any nourishment, since I left the encampment ; I had with me my gun and ammunition, and was therefore under no anxiety in regard to food. The snow lay about half a foot in depth.

My eyes were now employed upon the trees. When their tops leaned different ways, I looked to the moss, or to the branches ; and by connecting one with another, I found the means of travelling with some degree of confidence.   At four o'clock, in the afternoon, the sun, to my inexpressible joy, broke from the clouds, and I had now no further need of examining the trees.

In going down the side of a lofty hill, I saw a herd of red-deer approaching. Desirous of killing one of them for food, I hid myself in the bushes, and on a large one coming near, presented my piece, which missed fire, on account of the priming having been wetted.   The animals walked along, without taking the least alarm ; and, having re-loaded my gun, I followed them, and presented a second time.   But, now, a disaster of the heaviest kind had befallen me ; for, on attempting to fire, I found that I had lost the cock.   I had previously lost the screw by which it was fastened to the lock ; and to prevent this from being lost also, I had tied it in its place, with a leather string : the lock, to prevent its catching in the bows, I had carried under my molton coat.

Of all the sufferings which I had experienced, this seemed to me the most severe.   I was in a strange country, and knew not how far I had to go. I had been three days without food ; I was now without the means of procuring myself either food or fire.   Despair had almost overpowered me ; but, I soon resigned myself into the hands of that Providence, whose arm had so often saved me, and returned on my track, in search of what I had lost. My search was in vain, and I resumed my course, wet, cold and hungry, and almost without clothing.

CHAPTER XVII.

Author regains the Encampment—kills a Bear.
Indians endeavour to soothe the Manes of the
Bear, and pay it the homage of the customary
Feast. Some Remarks on the Natural History of
the Bear.   Stag-hunting.

THE sun was setting fast, when I descended a
hill, at the bottom of which was a small lake, entirely frozen over.   On drawing near, I saw a bea-
ver-lodge in the middle, offering some faint prospect
of food ; but, I found it already broken up. While
I looked at it, it suddenly occurred to me, that I
had seen it before ; and turning my eyes round the
place, I discovered a small tree, which I had myself
cut down, in the autumn, when, in company with
my friends, I had taken the beaver.   I was no
longer at a loss, but knew both the distance and
the route to the encampment.   The latter was only
to follow the course of a small stream of water,
which ran from the encampment to the lake on
which I stood. An hour before, I had thought myself the most miserable of men ; and now I leaped
for joy, and called myself the happiest.

The whole of the night, and through all the succeeding day, I walked up the rivulet, and at sun-
set reached the encampment, where I was received
with the warmest expressions of pleasure by the
family, by whom I had been given up for lost, after
a long and vain search for me in the woods.

Some days elapsed, during which I rested myself, and recruited my strength : after this, I resumed the chase, secure, that as the snow had
now fallen, I could always return by the way
I went.

In the course of the month of January, I happened to observe that the trunk of a very large
pine-tree was much torn by the claws of a bear,
made both in going up and down. On further
examination, I saw that there was a large opening,
in the upper part, near which the smaller branches
were broken. From these marks, and from the
additional circumstance, that there were no tracks
on the snow, there was reason to believe that a bear
lay concealed in the tree.

On returning to the lodge, I communicated my
discovery ; and it was agreed that all the family
should go together, in the morning, to assist in cutting down the tree, the girth of which was not less
than three fathom. The women, at first, opposed
the undertaking, because our axes, being only of a

pound and a half weight, were not well adapted to so heavy a labour ; but, the hope of finding a large bear, and obtaining from its fat a great quantity of oil, an article at the time much wanted, at length prevailed.

Accordingly, in the morning, we surrounded the tree, both men and women, as many at a time as could conveniently work at it ; and here we toiled, like beaver, till the sun went down. This day's work carried us about half way through the trunk ; and the next morning we renewed the attack, continuing it till about two o'clock, in the afternoon, when the tree fell to the ground. For a few minutes, every thing remained quiet, and I feared that all our expectations were disappointed ; but, as I advanced to the opening, there came out, to the great satisfaction of all our party, a bear of extraordinary size, which, before she had proceeded many yards, I shot.

The bear being dead, all my assistants approached, and all, but more particularly my old mother, (as I was wont to call her,) took his head in their hands, stroking and kissing it several times ; begging a thousand pardons for taking away her life ; calling her their relation and grandmother ; and requesting her not to lay the fault upon them, since it was truly an Englishman that had put her to death.

This ceremony was not of long duration ; and if it
was I that killed their grand-mother, they were not
themselves behind-hand in what remained to be
performed. The skin being taken off, we found the
fat in several places six inches deep. This, being
divided into two parts, loaded two persons; and the
flesh parts were as much as four persons could
carry.   In all, the carcass must have exceeded five
hundred weight.

As soon as we reached the lodge, the bear's head
was adorned with all the trinkets in the possession
of the family, such as silver arm-bands and wrist-
bands, and belts of wampum ; and then laid upon a
scaffold, set up for its reception, within the lodge.
Near the nose, was placed a large quantity of tobacco.

The next morning no sooner appeared, than preparations were made for a feast to the manes. The
lodge was cleaned and swept ; and the head of the
bear lifted up, and a new stroud blanket, which had
never been used before, spread under it. The pipes
were now lit ; and Wawatam blew tobacco-smoke
into the nostrils of the bear, telling me to do
the same, and thus appease the anger of the bear,
on account of my having killed her. I endeavoured to persuade my benefactor and friendly
adviser, that she no longer had any life, and assured him that I was under no apprehension from

her displeasure ; but, the first proposition obtained no credit, and the second gave but little satisfaction.

At length, the feast being ready, Wawatam
commenced a speech, resembling, in many things,
his address to the manes of his relations and departed companions ; but, having this peculiarity, that
he here deplored the necessity under which men
laboured, thus to destroy their *friends*. He represented, however, that the misfortune was unavoid-
able, since without doing so, they could by no
means subsist.   The speech ended, we all ate
heartily of the bear's flesh ; and even the head itself,
after remaining three days on the scaffold, was put
into the kettle.

It is only the female bear that makes her winter
lodging in the upper parts of trees, a practice by
which her young are secured from the attacks of
wolves and other animals.   She brings forth in the
winter-season ; and remains in her lodge till the
cubs have gained some strength.

The male always lodges in the ground, under the
roots of trees.   He takes to this habitation as soon
as the snow falls, and remains there till it has dis-
appeared. The Indians remark, that the bear comes

19

out in the spring with the same fat which he carried in, in the autumn ; but, after exercise of only a
few days, becomes lean. Excepting for a short part
of the season, the male lives constantly alone.

The fat of our bear was melted down, and the
oil filled six porcupine-skins.* A part of the meat
was cut into strips, and fire-dried, after which it was
put into the vessels containing the oil, where it remained in perfect preservation, until the middle of
summer.

February, in the country and by the people
where and among whom I was, is called the Moon
of Hard, or Crusted Snow ; for now the snow
can bear a man, or at least dogs, in pursuit of
animals of the chase. At this season, the stag is
very successfully hunted, his feet breaking through
at every step, and the crust upon the snow,
cutting his legs, with its sharp edges, to the
very bone. He is consequently, in this distress,
an easy prey ; and it frequently happened that
we killed twelve in the short space of two hours.
By this means, we were soon put into possession of four thousand weight of dried venison,

* The animal, which, in America, is called the porcupine,
is a hedge-hog, or urchin.

which was to be carried on our backs, along with all the rest of our wealth, for seventy miles, the distance of our encampment from that part of the lake shore, at which in the autumn we left our canoes. This journey it was our next business to perform.

CHAPTER XVIII.

Commence return to Michilimackinac. Join other Indian Families, and make Maple-sugar. Family Lands. Child Scalded. Prayers, Fasts and Sacrifices for its Recovery. Child Dies. Body carried for Burial, at the accustomed Burial-ground of the Family. Burial. Indian Opinions concerning the Future State of the Soul of Man.

OUR venison and furs and peltries were to be disposed of at Michilimackinac, and it was now the season for carrying them to market. The women therefore prepared our loads; and the morning of departure being come, we sat off at day-break, and continued our march till two o'clock in the afternoon. Where we stopped, we erected a scaffold, on which we deposited the bundles we had brought, and returned to our encampment, which we reached in the evening. In the morning, we carried fresh loads, which being deposited with the rest, we returned a second time in the evening. This we repeated, till all was forwarded one stage. Then, removing our lodge to the place of deposit, we carried our goods, with the same patient toil, a second

stage ; and so on, till we were at no great distance
from the shores of the lake.

Arrived here, we turned our attention to sugar-
making, the management of which, as I have before
related, belongs to the women, the men cutting
wood for the fires, and hunting and fishing.   In
the midst of this, we were joined by several lodges
of Indians, most of whom were of the family to
which I belonged, and had wintered near us.   The
lands belonged to this family, and it had therefore the exclusive right to hunt on them.   This
is according to the custom of the people ;   for
each family has its own lands.   I was treated very
civilly by all the lodges.

Our society had been a short time enlarged, by
this arrival of our friends, when an accident occurred which filled all the village with anxiety and sor-
row.   A little child, belonging to one of our neighbours, fell into a kettle of boiling syrup.   It was
instantly snatched out, but with little hope of its
recovery.

So long, however, as it lived, a continual feast
was observed ;   and this was made to the Great
Spirit and Master of Life, that he might be pleased
to save and heal the child.   At this feast, I was a
constant guest ;   and often found difficulty in eating
the large quantity of food, which, on such occa-

sions as these, is put upon each man's dish. The Indians accustom themselves both to eat much, and to fast much, with facility.

Several sacrifices were also offered; among which were dogs, killed and hung upon the tops of poles, with the addition of stroud blankets and other articles. These, also, were given to the Great Spirit, in humble hope that he would give efficacy to the medicines employed.

The child died. To preserve the body from the wolves, it was placed upon a scaffold, where it remained till we went to the lake, on the border of which was the burial-ground of the family.

On our arrival there, which happened in the beginning of April, I did not fail to attend the funeral. The grave was made of a large size, and the whole of the inside lined with birch-bark. On the bark was laid the body of the child, accompanied with an axe, a pair of snow-shoes, a small kettle, several pairs of common shoes, its own strings of beads, and—because it was a girl—a carrying-belt and a paddle. The kettle was filled with meat.

All this was again covered with bark ; and at about two feet nearer the surface, logs were laid across, and these again covered with bark, so that the earth might by no means fall upon the corpse.

The last act before the burial, performed by the mother, crying over the dead body of her child, was that of taking from it a lock of hair, for a memorial. While she did this, I endeavoured to console her, by offering the usual arguments; that the child was happy in being released from the miseries of this present life, and that she should forbear to grieve, because it would be restored to her in another world, happy and everlasting. She answered, that she knew it, and that by the lock of hair she should discover her daughter; for she would take it with her.—In this she alluded to the day, when some pious hand would place in her own grave, along with the carrying-belt and paddle, this little relic, hallowed by maternal tears.

I have frequently inquired into the ideas and opinions of the Indians, in regard to futurity, and always found that they were somewhat different, in different individuals.

Some suppose their souls to remain in this world, although invisible to human eyes; and capable, themselves, of seeing and hearing their friends, and also of assisting them, in moments of distress and danger.

Others dismiss from the mortal scene the unembodied spirit, and send it to a distant world or

country, in which it receives reward or punish-
ment, according to the life which it has led in its
prior state.   Those who have lived virtuously are
transported into a place abounding with every
luxury, with deer and all other animals of the woods
and water, and where the earth produces, in their
greatest perfection, all its sweetest fruits.   While,
on the other hand, those who have violated or neglected the duties of this life, are removed to a barren soil, where they wander up and down, among
rocks and morasses, and are stung by gnats, as
large as pigeons.

CHAPTER XIX.

Indians apprehensive of an attack from the En-
glish—kill a Panther—embark for Michili-
mackinac. Author consulted as to information
conveyed to him in Dreams—sells his Furs and
Peltries. Indian taciturnity. Author's Life
threatened. Wawatam carries him from Fort
Michilimackinac. Dreams of Wawatam's Wife
oblige the Family to remain at Isle aux Outardes.

WHILE we remained on the border of the lake,
a watch was kept every night, in the apprehension
of a speedy attack from the English, who were expected to avenge the massacre of Michilimackinac.
The immediate grounds of this apprehension were
the constant dreams, to this effect, of the more
aged women. I endeavoured to persuade them
that nothing of the kind would take place ; but
their fears were not to be subdued.

Amid these alarms, there came a report concerning a real, though less formidable enemy,
discovered in our neighbourhood. This was a

20

panther, which one of our young men had seen, and which animal sometimes attacks and carries away the Indian children. Our camp was immediately on the alert, and we set off into the woods, about twenty in number. We had not proceeded more than a mile, before the dogs found the panther, and pursued him to a tree, on which he was shot. He was of a large size.

On the twenty-fifth of April, we embarked for Michilimackinac. At La Grande Traverse, we met a large party of Indians, who appeared to labour, like ourselves, under considerable alarm; and who dared proceed no further, lest they should be destroyed by the English. Frequent councils of the united bands were held; and interrogations were continually put to myself, as to whether or not I knew of any design to attack them. I found that they believed it possible for me to have a fore-knowledge of events, and to be informed by dreams of all things doing at a distance.

Protestations of my ignorance were received with but little satisfaction, and incurred the suspicion of a design to conceal my knowledge. On this account therefore, or because I saw them tormented with fears which had nothing but imagination to rest upon, I told them, at length, that I knew there was no enemy to insult them; and that they

might proceed to Michilimackinac without danger
from the English,   I further, and with more confidence, declared, that if ever my countrymen returned to Michilimackihac, I would recommend
them to their favour, on account of the good treatment which I had received from them.   Thus encouraged, they embarked at an early hour the
next morning. In crossing the bay, we experienced
a storm of thunder and lightening.

Our port was the village of L'Arbre Croche,
which we reached in safety, and where we staid till
the following day.   At this village we found several persons who had been lately at Michilimackinac,
and from them we had the satisfaction of learning
that all was quiet there.   The remainder of our
voyage was therefore performed with confidence.

In the evening of the twenty-seventh, we landed
at the fort, which now contained only two French
traders.   The Indians who had arrived before us
were very few in number ; and by all who were of
our party, I was used very kindly.   I had the
entire freedom both of the fort and camp.

Wawatam and myself settled our stock, and paid
our debts ; and this done, I found that my share
of what was left consisted in a hundred beaver-
skins, sixty racoon-skins and six otter, of the

total value of about one hundred and sixty dollars. With these earnings of my winter's toil, I proposed to purchase clothes, of which I was much in need, having been six months without a shirt; but, on inquiring into the prices of goods, I found that all my funds would not go far. I was able, however, to buy two shirts, at ten pounds of beaver each ; a pair of *leggings*, or pantaloons, of scarlet cloth, which, with the ribbon to garnish them *fashionably*, cost me fifteen pounds of beaver; a blanket, at twenty pounds of beaver; and some other articles, at proportionable rates. In this manner, my wealth was soon reduced; but, not before I had laid in a good stock of ammunition and tobacco. To the use of the latter I had become much attached during the winter. It was my principal recreation, after returning from the chase; for my companions in the lodge were unaccustomed to pass the time in conversation. Among the Indians, the topics of conversation are but few, and limited for the most part, to the transactions of the day, the number of animals which they have killed, and of those which have escaped their pursuit; and other incidents of the chase. Indeed, the causes of taciturnity among the Indians, may be easily understood, if we consider how many occasions of speech, which present themselves to us, are utterly unknown to them ; the records of history, the pursuits of science, the disquisitions of philosophy, the systems

of politics, the business and the amusements of the
day, and the transactions of the four corners of
the world.

Eight days had passed in tranquillity, when
there arrived a band of Indians from the Bay of
Saguenaum.   They had assisted at the siege of
Détroit, and came to muster as many recruits for
that service as they could.   For my own part, I
was soon informed, that as I was the only Englishman in the place, they proposed to kill me, in order
to give their friends a mess of English broth, to
raise their courage.

This intelligence was not of the most agreeable
kind ; and in consequence of receiving it, I requested my friend to carry me to the Sault de
Sainte-Marie, at which place I knew the Indians to
be peaceably inclined, and that M. Cadotte enjoyed a powerful influence over their conduct.
They considered M. Cadotte as their chief ; and
he was not only my friend, but a friend to the English.   It was by him that the Chipeways of Lake
Superior were prevented from joining Pontiac.

Wawatam was not slow to exert himself for my
preservation ; but, leaving Michilimackinac in the

night, transported myself and all his lodge to Point
Saint-Ignace, on the opposite side of the strait.
Here we remained till day-light, and then went into
the Bay of Boutchitaouy, in which we spent three
days in fishing and hunting, and where we found
plenty of wild-fowl. Leaving the bay, we made
for the Isle aux Outardes, where we were obliged
to put in, on account of the wind's coming ahead.
We proposed sailing for the Sault the next
morning.

But, when the morning came, Wawatam's wife
complained that she was sick, adding, that she
had had bad dreams, and knew that if we went
to the Sault we should all be destroyed. To
have argued, at this time, against the infallibility
of dreams, would have been extremely unadvisa-
ble, since I should have appeared to be guilty, not
only of an odious want of faith, but also of a still
more odious want of sensibility to the possible calamities of a family which had done so much for
the alleviation of mine. I was silent; but the disappointment seemed to seal my fate. No prospect
opened to console me. To return to Michilimackinac could only ensure my destruction; and to
remain at the island was to brave almost equal danger, since it lay in the direct route between the fort

and the Missisaki, along which the Indians from
Détroit were hourly expected to pass, on the business of their mission.   I doubted not, but, taking
advantage of the solitary situation of the family,
they would carry into execution their design of
killing me.

CHAPTER XX.

Author is again relieved—takes leave of Wawatam and his Family—is hospitably received by M. Cadotte, at the Sault de Sainte-Marie—pursued by the Indians. Embassy from Sir William Johnson. Deputation to Sir William—Author to accompany it. GREAT TURTLE *to be consulted.*

UNABLE therefore to take any part in the direction of our course, but a prey at the same time to the most anxious thoughts as to my own condition, I passed all the day on the highest part, to which I could climb, of a tall tree, and whence the lake, on both sides of the island, lay open to my view. Here I might hope to learn, at the earliest possible, the approach of canoes, and by this means be warned in time to conceal myself.

On the second morning, I returned, as soon as it was light, to my watch-tower, on which I had not been long before I discovered a sail, coming from Michilimackinac.

The sail was a white one, and much larger than those usually employed by the Northern Indians. I therefore indulged a hope that it might be a Canadian canoe, on its voyage to Montréal; and that I might be able to prevail upon the crew to take me with them and thus release me from all my troubles.

My hopes continued to gain ground; for I soon persuaded myself that the manner in which the paddles were used, on board the canoe, was Canadian, and not Indian. My spirits were elated; but, disappointment had become so usual with me, that I could not suffer myself to look to the event with any strength of confidence.

Enough, however, appeared at length to demonstrate itself, to induce me to descend the tree, and repair to the lodge, with my tidings and schemes of liberty. The family congratulated me on the approach of so fair an opportunity of escape; and my father and brother, (for he was alternately each of these,) lit his pipe, and presented it to me, saying, " My son, this may be the last time that ever you " and I shall smoke out of the same pipe! I am " sorry to part with you. You know the affection " which I have always borne you, and the dangers " to which I have exposed myself and family, to " preserve you from your enemies; and I am hap-

" py to find that my efforts promise not to have
" been in vain."—At this time, a boy came into
the lodge, informing us that the canoe had come
from Michilimackinac, and was bound to the Sault
de Sainte-Marie.   It was manned by three Canadians, and was carrying home Madame Cadotte,
the wife of M. Cadotte, already mentioned.

My hopes of going to Montréal being now dissipated, I resolved on accompanying Madame Cadotte, with her permission, to the Sault.   On com-
municating my wishes to Madame Cadotte, she
cheerfully acceded to them.   Madame Cadotte, as
I have already mentioned, was an Indian woman,
of the Chipeway nation ; and she was very generally respected.

My departure fixed upon, I returned to the
lodge, where I packed up my wardrobe, consisting
of my two shirts, pair of *leggings* and blanket.
Besides these, I took a gun and ammunition, presenting what remained further to my host.   I also
returned the silver arm-bands, with which the family had decorated me, the year before.

We now exchanged farewells, with an emotion
entirely reciprocal. I did not quit the lodge without
the most grateful sense of the many acts of good-
ness which I had experienced in it, nor without the

sincerest respect for the virtues which I had witnessed among its members. All the family accompanied me to the beach ; and the canoe had no
sooner put off, than Wawatam commenced an address to the Ki'chi' Ma'ni'to', beseeching him to
take care of me, his brother, till we should next
meet. This, he had told me, would not be long,
as he intended to return to Michilimackinac for a
short time only, and would then follow me to the
Sault.—We had proceeded to too great a distance
to allow of our hearing his voice, before Wawatam
had ceased to offer up his prayers.

Being now no longer in the society of Indians, I
laid aside the dress, putting on that of a Canadian :
a molton or blanket coat, over my shirt ; and a
handkerchief about my head, hats being very little
worn in this country.

At day-break, on the second morning of our
voyage, we embarked, and presently perceived several canoes behind us. As they approached, we
ascertained them to be the fleet, bound for the Missisaki, of which I had been so long in dread. It
amounted to twenty sail.

On coming up with us, and surrounding our
canoe, and amid general inquiries concerning the
news, an Indian challenged me for an Englishman,
and his companions supported him, by declaring

that I looked very like one ; but I affected not to understand any of the questions which they asked me, and Madâme Cadotte assured them that I was a Canadian, whom she had brought on his first voyage from Montréal.

The following day saw us safely landed at the Sault, where I experienced a generous welcome from M. Cadotte. There were thirty warriors at this place, restrained from joining in the war only by M. Cadotte's influence.

Here, for five days, I was once more in possession of tranquillity ; but, on the sixth, a young Indian came into M. Cadotte's, saying that a canoe full of warriors had just arrived from Michilimack·inac ; that they had inquired for me ; and that he believed their intentions to be bad. Nearly at the same time, a message came from the good chief of the village, desiring me to conceal myself, until he should discover the views and temper of the strangers.

A garret was a second time my place of refuge ; and it was not long before the Indians came to M. Cadotte's. My friend immediately informed Mut'chi'ki'wish', their chief, who was related to his wife, of the design imputed to them, of mischief against myself. Mutchikiwish frankly acknowledged that they had had such a design ; but added that if displeasing to M. Cadotte, it should be abandoned.   He then further stated, that their errand was to raise a party of warriors to return with them to Détroit ; and that it had been their intention to take me with them.

In regard to the principal of the two objects thus disclosed, M. Cadotte proceeded to assemble all the chiefs and warriors of the village ; and these, after deliberating for some time among themselves, sent for the strangers, to whom both M. Cadotte and the chief of the village addressed a speech.   In these speeches, after recurring to the designs con-fessed to have been entertained against myself, who was now declared to be under the immediate pro-tection of all the chiefs, by whom any insult I might sustain would be avenged, the ambassadors were peremptorily told, that they might go back, as they came, none of the young men of this village being foolish enough to join them.

A moment after, a report was brought, that a ca-noe had just arrived from Niagara.   As this was a place from which every one was anxious to hear news, a message was sent to these fresh strangers, requesting them to come to the council.

The strangers came accordingly, and being seat-ed, a long silence ensued.   At length, one of them, taking up a belt of wampum, addressed himself thus to the assembly :   " My friends and brothers, " I am come, with this belt, from our great father,

" Sir William Johnson. He desired me to come
" to you, as his ambassador, and tell you, that he is
" making a great feast at Fort Niagara ; that his
" kettles are all ready, and his fires lit. He invites
" you to partake of the feast, in common with your
" friends, the Six Nations, which have all made
" peace with the English. He advises you to seize
" this opportunity of doing the same, as you cannot
" otherwise fail of being destroyed ; for the En-
" glish are on their march, with a great army, which
" will be joined by different nations of Indians. In
" a word, before the fall of the leaf, they will be at
" Michilimackinac, and the Six Nations with
" them."

The tenor of this speech greatly alarmed the
Indians of the Sault, who, after a very short consultation, agreed to send twenty deputies to Sir
William Johnson, at Niagara. This was a project
highly interesting to me, since it offered me the
means of leaving the country. I intimated this to
the chief of the village, and received his promise
that I should accompany the deputation.

Very little time was proposed to be lost, in setting forward on the voyage; but, the occasion was
of too much magnitude not to call for more than
human knowledge and discretion ; and preparations were accordingly made for solemnly invoking
and consulting the GREAT TURTLE.

CHAPTER XXI.

Preparations for invoking the GREAT TURTLE.—
*His voice is heard—He is questioned. His re-
plies. Voyage to Fort Niagara commenced.*

FOR invoking and consulting the Great Turtle,
the first thing to be done was the building of a large
house or wigwam, within which was placed a species of tent, for the use of the priest, and reception
of the spirit. The tent was formed of moose-
skins, hung over a frame-work of wood. Five
poles, or rather pillars, of five different species of
timber, about ten feet in height, and eight inches
in diameter, were set in a circle of about four feet
in diameter. The holes made to receive them were
about two feet deep; and the pillars being set,
the holes were filled up again, with the earth which
had been dug out. At top, the pillars were bound
together by a circular hoop, or girder. Over the
whole of this edifice were spread the moose-skins,
covering it at top and round the sides, and made
fast with thongs of the same; except that on one
side a part was left unfastened, to admit of the entrance of the priest.

The ceremonies did not commence but with the approach of night. To give light within the house, several fires were kindled round the tent. Nearly the whole village assembled in the house, and myself among the rest. It was not long before the priest appeared, almost in a state of nakedness. As he approached the tent the skins were lifted up, as much as was necessary to allow of his creeping under them, on his hands and knees. His head was scarcely within side, when the edifice, massy as it has been described, began to shake ; and the skins were no sooner let fall, than the sounds of numerous voices were heard beneath them ; some yelling ; some barking as dogs ; some howling like wolves : and in this horrible concert were mingled screams and sobs, as of despair, anguish and the sharpest pain. Articulate speech was also uttered, as if from human lips ; but in a tongue unknown to any of the audience.

After some time, these confused and frightful noises were succeeded by a perfect silence ; and now a voice, not heard before, seemed to manifest the arrival of a new character in the tent. This was a low and feeble voice, resembling the cry of a young puppy. The sound was no sooner distinguished, than all the Indians clapped their hands for joy, exclaiming, that this was the Chief Spirit, the TUR-TLE, the spirit that never lied! Other voices, which they had discriminated from time to time, they had previously hissed, as recognising them to belong to evil and lying spirits, which deceive mankind.

New sounds came from the tent. During the space of half an hour, a succession of songs were heard, in which a diversity of voices met the ear. From his first entrance, till these songs were finished, we heard nothing in the proper voice of the priest; but, now, he addressed the multitude, declaring the presence of the GREAT TURTLE, and the spirit's readiness to answer such questions as should be proposed.

The questions were to come from the chief of the village, who was silent, however, till after he had put a large quantity of tobacco into the tent, introducing it at the aperture. This was a sacrifice, offered to the spirit; for spirits are supposed by the Indians to be as fond of tobacco as themselves. The tobacco accepted, he desired the priest to inquire, Whether or not the English were preparing to make war upon the Indians? and, Whether or not there were at Fort Niagara a large number of English troops?

These questions having been put by the priest, the tent instantly shook; and for some seconds after, it continued to rock so violently, that I ex-

22

pected to see it levelled with the ground. All this was a prelude, as I supposed, to the answers to be given ; but, a terrific cry announced, with sufficient intelligibility, the departure of the Tur-tle.

A quarter of an hour elapsed in silence, and I waited impatiently to discover what was to be the next incident, in this scene of imposture. It con-sisted in the return of the spirit, whose voice was again heard, and who now delivered a continued speech. The language of the Great Turtle, like that which we had heard before, was wholly unintelligible to every ear, that of his priest ex-cepted ; and it was, therefore, that not till the latter gave us an interpretation, which did not commence before the spirit had finished, that we learned the purport of this extraordinary commu-nication.

The spirit, as we were now informed by the priest, had, during his short absence, crossed Lake Huron, and even proceeded as far as Fort Niagara, which is at the head of Lake Ontario, and thence to Montréal. At Fort Niagara, he had seen no great number of soldiers ; but, on descending the Saint Lawrence, as low as Montréal, he had found the river covered with boats, and the boats filled with soldiers, in number like the leaves of the trees. He had met them on their way up the river, coming to make war upon the Indians.

The chief had a third question to propose, and the spirit, without a fresh journey to Fort Niagara, was able to give it an instant and most favourable answer: " If," said the chief, " the Indians visit " Sir William Johnson, will they be received as " friends ?"

" Sir William Johnson," said the spirit, (and after the spirit, the priest,) " Sir William Johnson " will fill their canoes with presents; with blankets, " kettles, guns, gun-powder and shot, and large " barrels of rum, such as the stoutest of the In- " dians will not be able to lift ; and every man will " return in safety to his family."

At this, the transport was universal ; and, amid the clapping of hands, a hundred voices exclaimed, " I will go, too ! I will go, too !"

The questions of public interest being resolved, individuals were now permitted to seize the opportunity of inquiring into the condition of their absent friends, and the fate of such as were sick. I observed that the answers, given to these questions, allowed of much latitude of inter, pretation.

Amid this general inquisitiveness, I yielded to the solicitations of my own anxiety for the future ; and having first, like the rest, made my offering of tobacco, I inquired, whether or not I should ever revisit my native country ?   The question being put by the priest, the tent shook as usual ; after which I received this answer :   " That I " should take courage, and fear no danger, for that " nothing would happen to hurt me ; and that I " should, in the end, reach my friends and country " in safety."   These assurances wrought so strongly on my gratitude, that I presented an additional and extra offering of tobacco.

The GREAT TURTLE continued to be consulted till near midnight, when all the crowd dispersed to their respective lodges.   I was on the watch, through the scene I have described, to detect the particular contrivances by which the fraud was carried on ; but, such was the skill displayed in the performance, or such my deficiency of penetration, that I made no discoveries, but came away as I went, with no more than those general surmises which will naturally be entertained by every reader.*

* M. de Champlain has left an account of an exhibition of the nature here described, which may be seen in Charlevoix's Histoire et Description Generale de la Nouvelle France, livre IV. This took place in the year 1609, and was performed among a party of warriors, composed of Al-

On the 10th of June, I embarked with the Indian deputation, composed of sixteen men. Twenty had been the number originally designed; and upward of fifty actually engaged themselves to the council for the undertaking ; to say nothing of the general enthusiasm, at the moment of hearing the GREAT TURTLE'S promises. But, exclusively of the degree of timidity which still prevailed, we are to take into account the various domestic calls, which might supersede all others, and detain many with their families.

gonquins, Montagnez and Hurons. Carver witnessed another, among the Cristinaux. In each case, the details are somewhat different, but the outline is the same. M. de Champlain mentions, that he saw the *jongleur* shake the stakes or pillars of the tent. I was not so fortunate ; but, this is the obvious explanation of that part of the mystery to which it refers. Captain Carver leaves the whole in darkness.

CHAPTER XXII.

Voyage from the Sault de Sainte-Marie to Niagara.
Hospitable reception from the Missisakies. Au-
thor alarmed by a Rattle-snake—and is about to
kill it. Indians interfere—declare it to be a
Manito—treat it accordingly. Inoffensive de-
meanour of the Rattle-snake. Indians appre-
hend some evil from the Author's crime against
the Manito. Overtaken by a gale of wind.
Prayers and Sacrifices to the Rattle-snake. Ar-
rive at Fort Niagara.

IN the evening of the second day of our voyage,
we reached the mouth of the Missisaki, where we
found about forty Indians, by whom we were
received with abundant kindness, and at night
regaled at a great feast, held on account of our
arrival. The viand was a preparation of the roe of
the sturgeon, beat up, and boiled, and of the con-
sistence of porridge.

After eating, several speeches were made to us,
of which the general topic was a request, that we

should recommend the village to Sir William Johnson. This request was also specially addressed to me, and I promised to comply with it.

On the 14th of June, we passed the village of La Cloche, of which the greater part of the inhabitants were absent, being already on a visit to Sir William Johnson. This circumstance greatly encouraged the companions of my voyage, who now saw that they were not the first to run into danger.

The next day, about noon, the wind blowing very hard, we were obliged to put ashore at Point aux Grondines, a place of which some description has been given above. While the Indians erected a hut, I employed myself in making a fire. As I was gathering wood, an unusual sound fixed my attention for a moment; but, as it presently ceased, and as I saw nothing from which I could suppose it to proceed, I continued my employment, till, advancing further, I was alarmed by a repetition. I imagined that it came from above my head; but, after looking that way in vain, I cast my eyes on the ground, and there discovered a rattlesnake, at not more than two feet from my naked legs. The reptile was coiled, and its head raised considerably above its body. Had I advanced another step before my discovery, I must have trodden upon it.

I no sooner saw the snake, than I hastened to the canoe, in order to procure my gun ; but, the Indians observing what I was doing, inquired the occasion, and being informed, begged me to desist. At the same time, they followed me to the spot, with their pipes and tobacco-pouches in their hands. On returning, I found the snake still coiled.

The Indians, on their part, surrounded it, all addressing it by turns, and calling it their *grand-father ;* but yet keeping at some distance. During this part of the ceremony, they filled their pipes ; and now each blew the smoke toward the snake, who, as it appeared to me, really received it with pleasure. In a word, after remaining coiled, and receiving incense, for the space of half an hour, it stretched itself along the ground, in visible good humour. Its length was between four and five feet. Having remained outstretched for some time, at last it moved slowly away, the Indians following it, and still addressing it by the title of grand-father, beseeching it to take care of their families during their absence, and to be pleased to open the heart of Sir William Johnson, so that he might *show them charity*, and fill their canoe with rum.

One of the chiefs added a petition, that the snake would take no notice of the insult which had been offered him by the Englishman, who would even have put him to death, but for the interference of the Indians, to whom it was hoped he would impute no part of the offence. They further requested, that he would remain, and inhabit their country, and not return among the English ; that is, go eastward.

After the rattle-snake was gone, I learned that this was the first time that an individual of the species had been seen so far to the northward and westward of the river Des Français ; a circumstance, moreover, from which my companions were disposed to infer, that this *manito* had come, or been sent, on purpose to meet them ; that his errand had been no other than to stop them on their way ; and that consequently it would be most advisable to return to the point of departure. I was so fortunate, however, as to prevail with them to embark ; and at six o'clock in the evening we again encamped. Very little was spoken of through the evening, the rattle-snake excepted.

Early the next morning we proceeded. We had a serene sky and very little wind, and the Indians therefore determined on steering across the lake, to an island which just appeared in the horizon ; saving, by this course, a distance of thirty miles, which would be lost in keeping the shore.

23

At nine o'clock, A. M. we had a light breeze astern, to enjoy the benefit of which we hoisted sail. Soon after, the wind increased, and the Indians, beginning to be alarmed, frequently called on the rattle-snake to come to their assistance. By degrees the waves grew high ; and at 11 o'clock it blew a hurricane, and we expected every moment to be swallowed up. From prayers, the Indians now proceeded to sacrifices, both alike offered to the god-rattlesnake, or *manito-kinibic*. One of the chiefs took a dog, and after tying its fore legs together, threw it overboard, at the same time calling on the snake to preserve us from being drowned, and desiring him to satisfy his hunger with the carcass of the dog. The snake was unpropitious, and the wind increased. Another chief sacrificed another dog, with the addition of some tobacco. In the prayer which accompanied these gifts, he besought the snake, as before, not to avenge upon the Indians the insult which he had received from myself, in the conception of a design to put him to death. He assured the snake, that I was absolutely an Englishman, and of kin neither to him nor to them.

At the conclusion of this speech, an Indian, who sat near me, observed, that if we were drowned it would be for my fault alone, and that I ought myself to be sacrificed, to appease the angry manito ;

nor was I without apprehensions, that in case of extremity, this would be my fate ; but, happily for
me, the storm at length abated, and we reached the
island safely.

The next day was calm, and we arrived at the
entrance* of the navigation which leads to Lake
aux Claies.† We presently passed two short carrying-places, at each of which were several lodges
of Indians,‡ containing only women and children,
the men being gone to the council at Niagara.
From this, as from a former instance, my companions derived new courage.

On the 18th of June, we crossed Lake aux
Claies, which appeared to be upward of twenty
miles in length.   At its further end, we came to
the carrying-place of Toranto.§   Here the In-

* This is the Bay of Matchedash, or Matchitashk.

† This lake, which is now called Lake Simcoe, lies between Lakes Huron and Ontario.

‡ These Indians are Chipeways, of the particular description called Missisakies ; and from their residence at Matchedash, or Matchitashk, also called Matchedash, or Matchitashk Indians.

§ Toranto, or Toronto, is the name of a French trading-
house, on Lake Ontario, built near the site of the present
town of York, the capital of the province of Upper Canada.

dians obliged me to carry a burden of more than a hundred pounds weight. The day was very hot, and the woods and marshes abounded with mosquitoes; but, the Indians walked at a quick pace, and I could by no means see myself left behind. The whole country was a thick forest, through which our only road was a foot-path, or such as, in America, is exclusively termed an *Indian path.*

Next morning, at ten o'clock, we reached the shore of Lake Ontario. Here we were employed two days in making canoes, out of the bark of the elm-tree, in which we were to transport ourselves to Niagara. For this purpose, the Indians first cut down a tree ; then stripped off the bark, in one entire sheet, of about eighteen feet in length, the incision being lengthwise. The canoe was now complete, as to its top, bottom and sides. Its ends were next closed, by sewing the bark together ; and a few ribs and bars being introduced, the architecture was finished. In this manner, we made two canoes ; of which one carried eight men, and the other, nine.

On the 21st, we embarked at Toranto, and encamped, in the evening, four miles short of Fort Niagara, which the Indians would not approach till morning.

At dawn, the Indians were awake, and presently assembled in council, still doubtful as to the fate they were to encounter. I assured them of the most friendly welcome ; and at length, after painting themselves with the most lively colours, in token of their own peaceable views, and after singing the song which is in use among them on going into danger, they embarked, and made for Point Missisaki, which is on the north side of the mouth of the river or strait of Niagara, as the fort is on the south. A few minutes after, I crossed over to the fort ; and here I was received by Sir William Johnson, in a manner for which I have ever been gratefully attached to his person, and memory.

Thus was completed my escape, from the sufferings and dangers which the capture of Fort Michilimackinac brought upon me ; but, the property which I had carried into the upper country was left behind. The reader will therefore be far from attributing to me any idle or unaccountable motive, when he finds me returning to the scene of my misfortunes.

CHAPTER XXIII.

Army, under General Bradstreet, prepares to raise the Siege of Détroit. Author induced to join, and set out, a second time, for Michilimackinac—appointed to the command of an Indian Corps. Siege of Détroit raised. General Peace with the Indians. Detachment garrisons Fort Michilimackinac. Author visits the Sault de Sainte-Marie—returns to Michilimackinac.

AT Fort Niagara, I found General Bradstreet, with a force of three thousand men, preparing to embark for Détroit, with a view to raise the siege which it had sustained against Pontiac, for twelve months together. The English, in this time, had lost many men ; and Pontiac had been frequently on the point of carrying the place, though gallantly defended by Major Gladwyn, its commandant.

General Bradstreet, having learned my history, informed me, that it was his design, on arriving at Détroit, to detach a body of troops to Michilimackinac, and politely assured me of his services, in recovering my property there.   With these temptations before me, I was easily induced to fol-low the general to Détroit.

But, I was not to go as a mere looker-on.   On the contrary, I was invested with the honour of a command in a corps, of the exploits, however, of which, I can give no very flattering account.

Besides the sixteen Saulteurs, or Chipeways of the Sault de Sainte-Marie, with whom I had come to Fort Niagara, there were already at that place eighty Matchedash Indians, the same whose lodges we passed, at the carrying-places of Lake aux Claies.   These ninety-six men being formed into what was called the Indian Battalion, were furnish-ed with necessaries ;   and I was appointed to be their leader—me, whose best hope it had very lately been, to live through their forbearance.

On the 10th of July, the army marched for Fort Schlausser, a stockaded post above the Great Falls ; and I ordered my Indians to march also. Only ten, of the whole number, were ready at the call ; but the rest promised to follow the next morning. With my skeleton-battalion, therefore, I proceeded to the fort, and there waited the whole of the next day, impatiently expecting the remainder. I waited in vain ; and the day following returned to Fort Nia-gara, when I found that they had all deserted, going

back to their homes, equipments and all, by
the way of Toranto. I thought their conduct,
though dishonest, not very extraordinary; since
the Indians employed in the siege of Détroit,
against whom we were leading them, were at
peace with their nation, and their own friends and
kinsmen.—Amid the general desertion, four Missisakies joined the ten whom I had left at Fort
Schlausser.

For the transport of the army, on Lake Erie,
barges had been expressly built, capable of carrying a hundred men each, with their provisions.
One of these was allowed to me and my Indians.

On the 14th, we embarked at Fort Schlausser,
and in the evening encamped at Fort Erie. Here
the Indians growing drunk, amused themselves
with a disorderly firing of their muskets, in the
camp. On this, General Bradstreet ordered all the
rum in the Indian quarters to be seized, and thrown
away. The Indians, in consequence, threatened
to desert; and the general, judging it proper to
assume a high tone, immediately assembled the
chiefs, (for, among the fourteen Indians, there were
more chiefs than one,) and told them, that he had
no further occasion for their services, and that such
of them as should follow his camp, would be considered as soldiers, and subjected to military discipline accordingly. After hearing the general's

speech, the majority set out for Fort Niagara, the same evening, and thence returned to their own country, by the way of Toranto ; and thus was my poor battalion still further diminished !

On our fifth day from Fort Schlausser, we reached Presqu'isle, where we dragged our barges over the neck of land, but not without straining their timbers ; and with more loss of time, as I believe, than if we had rowed round. On the twentieth day, we were off the mouth of the river which falls into Sandusky Bay, where a council of war was held, on the question, whether it were more advisable to attack and destroy the Indian villages, on the Miami, or to proceed for Détroit direct. Early the next morning, it having been determined, that considering the villages were populous, as well as hostile, it was necessary to destroy them, we entered the Miami ; but were presently met by a deputation, offering peace. The offer was accepted ; but it was not till after two days, during which we had begun to be doubtful of the enemy's intention, that the chiefs arrived. When they came, a sort of armistice was agreed upon ; and they promised to meet the general at Détroit, within fifteen days. At that place, terms of peace were to be settled, in a general council. On the 8th of August, we landed at Détroit.

The Indians of the Miami were punctual; and a general peace was concluded. Pontiac, who could do nothing against the force which was now opposed to him, and who saw himself abandoned by his followers, unwilling to trust his fortunes with the English, fled to the Illinois.*

On the day following that of the treaty of peace, Captain Howard was detached, with two companies, and three hundred Canadian volun-

---

* It is very possible, nevertheless, that Pontiac subsequently joined the English, and that a portion of what is related by Carver, concerning his latter history and death, is true. It cannot, however, be intended to insinuate, that an English governor was party to the assassination:

" Pontiac henceforward seemed to have laid aside the " animosity he had hitherto borne towards the English, and " apparently became their zealous friend. To reward this " new attachment, and to insure a continuance of it, govern- " ment allowed him a handsome pension. But his restless " and intriguing spirit would not suffer him to be grateful " for this allowance, and his conduct at length grew suspi- " cious; so that going, in the year 1767, to hold a council " in the country of the Illinois, a faithful Indian, who was " either commissioned by one of the English governors, or " instigated by the love he bore the English nation, attended " him as a spy; and being convinced from the speech Pon- " tiac made in the council, that he still retained his former " prejudices against those for whom he now professed a " friendship, he plunged his knife into his heart, as soon as " he had done speaking, and laid him dead on the spot."

teers, for Fort Michilimackinac ; and I embarked
at the same time.

From Détroit, to the mouth of Lake Huron,
is called a distance of eighty miles. From the
fort to Lake Sainte-Claire, which is only seven
miles, the lands are cultivated on both sides the
strait, and appeared to be laid out in very comfortable farms. In the strait, on the right hand, is
a village of Hurons, and at the mouth of Lake
Sainte-Claire, a village of Otawas. We met not a
single Indian on our voyage, the report of the
arrival of the English army having driven every
one from the shores of the lake.

On our arrival at Michilimackinac, the Otawas
of L'Arbre Croche were sent for to the fort. They
obeyed the summons, bringing with them some
Chipeway chiefs, and peace was concluded with
both.

For myself, having much property due to me at
Sainte-Marie's, I resolved on spending the winter
at that place. I was in part successful; and in the
spring I returned to Michilimackinac.

THE pause, which I shall here make in my narrative, might with some propriety have been pla-

ced at the conclusion of the preceding chapter ;
but, it is here that my first series of adventures are
brought truly to an end.   What remains, belongs
to a second enterprize, wholly independent on the
preceding.

END OF PART THE FIRST.

PART THE SECOND.

TRAVELS

AND ADVENTURES,

&c. &c.

PART THE SECOND.

———

CHAPTER I.

Fur-trade permitted only to licensed and privileged persons. Author obtains the exclusive trade of Lake Superior. Further commercial details of Michilimackinac. Author proceeds to the Sault de Sainte-Marie—embarks for his Wintering-ground at Chagouemig. Grave of the Iroquois —tradition. River Ontonagan—Sturgeon-fishery—and Copper. Indians beat the Copper into Spoons, Bracelets, &c. Chagouemig—distressed state of Indians there. Indians supplied— go to the chase.

UNDER the French government of Canada, the fur-trade was subject to a variety of regulations, established and enforced by the royal authority ; and, in 1765, the period at which I began to proseeute it anew, some remains of the ancient system were still preserved.   No person could go into the countries lying north-westward of Détroit, unless furnished with a license ; and the exclusive trade of particular districts was capable of being enjoyed, in virtue of grants from military commanders.

The exclusive trade of Lake Superior was given to myself, by the commandant of Fort Michili. mackinac ; and to prosecute it, I purchased goods, which I found at this post, at twelve months' credit. My stock was the freight of four canoes, and I took it at the price of ten thousand pounds weight of good and merchantable beaver.   It is in beaver that accounts are kept at Michilimackinac ; but in defect of this article, other furs and skins are accepted in payments, being first reduced unto their value in beaver.   Beaver was at this time at the price of two shillings and sixpence per pound, Michilimackinac-currency ;   otter skins, at six shillings each; marten, at one shilling and sixpence, and others in proportion.

To carry the goods to my wintering-ground in Lake Superior, I engaged twelve men, at two hundred and fifty livres, of the same currency, each ; that is, a hundred pounds weight of beaver.   For provisions, I purchased fifty bushels of maize, at ten pounds of beaver per bushel.   At this place, specie was so wholly out of the question, that in going to a cantine, you took with you a marten's skin, to pay your reckoning.*

On the 14th of July, 1765, I embarked for the Sault de Sainte-Marie, where, on my arrival, I took into partnership M. Cadotte, whom I have already had frequent occasion to name ; and on the 26th I proceeded for my wintering-ground, which was to be fixed at Chagouemig.

The next morning, I crossed the Strait of Sainte-Marie, or of Lake Superior, to a point, which the Chipeways call the Grave of the Iroquois. To this name there belongs a tradition, that the Iroquois, who, at a certain time, made war upon the Chipeways, with the design of dispossessing them of their country, encamped, one night, a thousand strong, upon this point; where, thinking themselves secure from their numbers, they indulged in feasting on the bodies of their prisoners. The sight, however, of the sufferings and humiliation of their kindred and friends, so wrought upon the Chipeways, who beheld them from the opposite shore, that with the largest number of warriors they could collect, but which amounted only to three hundred, they crossed the channel, and at break of day fell upon the Iroquois, now sleeping after their excesses,

* See Part I. Chapter 5.

25

and put one and all to death.   Of their own party,
they lost but a single man ; and he died of a wound
which he received from an old woman, who stabbed
him with an awl.   She was at work, making shoes
for the family, when he broke into the lodge, near
the entrance of which she sat.—Some of the old
men of my crew remembered at this place to have
seen bones.

On the lake, we fell in with Indians, of whom I
purchased provisions. One party agreed to accompany me, to hunt for me, on condition of being
supplied with necessaries on credit.

On the 19th of August, we reached the mouth
of the river Ontonagan, one of the largest on the
south side of the lake.   At the mouth, was an Indian village ; and at three leagues above, a fall,
at the foot of which sturgeon were at this season so
abundant, that a month's subsistence for a regiment could have been taken in a few hours.

But, I found this river chiefly remarkable for the
abundance of virgin copper, which is on its banks and
in its neighbourhood, and of which the reputation
is at present more generally spread, than it was at
the time of this my first visit. The attempts, which
were shortly after made, to work the mines of Lake
Superior to advantage, will very soon claim a place,
among the facts which I am to describe.

The copper presented itself to the eye, in masses of various weight. The Indians showed me one of twenty pounds. They were used to manufacture this metal into spoons and bracelets for themselves. In the perfect state in which they found it, it required nothing but to be beat into shape. The Pi-wâ-tic, or Iron-river, enters the lake to the westward of the Ontonagan; and here, as is pretended, silver was found, while the country was in the possession of the French.

Beyond this river, I met more Indians, whom I furnished with merchandise on credit. The prices were for a stroud blanket, ten beaver-skins; for a white blanket, eight; a pound of powder, two; a pound of shot, or of ball, one; a gun, twenty; an axe, of one pound weight, two; a knife, one.— Beaver, it will be remembered, was worth, at Michilimackinac, two shillings and sixpence a pound, in the currency of that place; that is, six livres, or a dollar.

On my arrival at Chagouemig, I found fifty lodges of Indians there. These people were almost naked, their trade having been interrupted, first by the English invasion of Canada, and next by Pontiac's war.

Adding the Indians of Chagouemig to those which I had brought with me, I had now a hundred

families, to all of whom I was required to advance
goods on credit.   At a council, which I was invited to attend, the men declared, that unless their
demands were complied with, their wives and children would perish ; for that there were neither ammunition nor clothing left among them.   Under
these circumstances, I saw myself obliged to dis-
tribute goods, to the amount of three thousand
beaver-skins.   This done, the Indians went on
their hunt, at the distance of a hundred leagues.
A clerk, acting as my agent, accompanied them to
Fond du Lac, taking with him two loaded canoes.
Meanwhile, at the expense of six days' labour, I
was provided with a very comfortable house, for
my winter's residence.

CHAPTER II.

Chagouemig. Hunt. Feast of Sacrifice to the Great Spirit—motives—and mode. Ludicrous incident. Comment of the Indians. Chipeway Campaign against the Nadowessies. Scalping the killed in battle esteemed honourable to the Nation to whom they belong. Author leaves Chagouemig—further explores the Banks of the Ontonagan.

CHAGOUEMIG, or Chagouemigon, might at this period be regarded as the metropolis of the Chipeways, of whom the true name is *O'chibbuoy*. The chiefs informed me, that they had frequently attacked the Nadowessies, (by the French called *Sioux* or *Nadouessioux*,) with whom they are always at war, with fifteen hundred men, including in this number the fighting-men from Fond du Lac, or the head of Lake Superior. The cause of the perpetual war, carried on between these two nations, is this, that both claim, as their exclusive hunting-ground, the tract of country which lies between them, and uniformly attack each other when they meet upon it.

The Chipeways of Chagouemig are a handsome well-made people ; and much more cleanly, as well as much more regular in the government of their families, than the Chipeways of Lake Huron. The women have agreeable features, and take great pains in dressing their hair, which consists in neatly dividing it on the forehead and top of the head, and in plaiting and turning it up behind. The men paint as well their whole body as their face ; sometimes with charcoal, and sometimes with white ochre ; and appear to study how to make themselves as unlike as possible to any thing human. The clothing, in which I found them, both men and women, was chiefly of dressed deer-skin, European manufactures having been for some time out of their reach. In this respect, it was not long, after my goods were dispersed among them, before they were scarcely to be known, for the same people. The women heightened the colour of their cheeks, and really animated their beauty, by a liberal use of vermilion.

My house being completed, my winter's food was the next object ; and for this purpose, with the assistance of my men, I soon took two thousand trout and white-fish, the former frequently weighing fifty pounds each, and the latter commonly from four to six. We preserved them by suspending them by the tail in the open air. These, without bread or salt, were our food through all the winter; the men being free to consume what quantity they pleased, and boiling or roasting them whenever they thought proper. After leaving Michilimackinac, I saw no bread ; and I found less difficulty, in reconciling myself to the privation, than I could have anticipated.

On the 15th of December, the Bay of Chagouemig was frozen entirely over. After this, I resumed my former amusement of spearing trout, and sometimes caught a hundred of these fish in a day, each weighing, on an average, twenty pounds.

My house, which stood in the bay, was sheltered by an island of fifteen miles in length, and between which and the main the channel is four miles broad. On the island, there was formerly a French trading-post, much frequented ; and in its neighbourhood a large Indian village. To the southeast is a lake, called Lake des Outaouais, from the Otawas, its former possessors ; but it is now the property of the Chipeways.

From the first hunting-party which brought me furs, I experienced some disorderly behaviour; but happily without serious issue. Having crowded into my house, and demanded rum, which I refused them, they talked of indulging themselves in a general pillage, and I found myself abandoned by all my men. Fortunately, I was able to arm myself; and on my threatening to shoot the first who should lay his hands on any thing, the tumult began to subside, and was presently after at an end. When over, my men appeared to be truly ashamed of their cowardice, and made promises never to behave in a similar manner again.

Admonished of my danger, I now resolved on burying the liquor which I had ; and the Indians, once persuaded that I had none to give them, went and came very peaceably, paying their debts and purchasing goods. In the month of March, the manufacture of maple-sugar engaged as usual their attention.

While the snow still lay on the ground, I proposed to the Indians to join me in a hunting excursion, and they readily agreed. Shortly after we went out, my companions discovered dents or hollows in the snow, which they affirmed to be the footsteps of a bear, made in the beginning of the winter, after the first snow.—As for me, I should have passed over the same ground without acquiring any such information ; and probably without remarking the very faint traces which they were able to distinguish, and certainly without deducing so many particular facts : but, what can be more credible, than that long habits of close observation in the forest, should give the Indian hunter some advantages, in the exercise of his daily calling? The Indians were not deceived ; for, on following the traces which they had found, they were led to a tree, at the root of which was a bear.

As I had proposed this hunt, I was, by the Indian custom, the master and the proprietor of all the game; but, the head of the family which composed my party begged to have the bear, alleging, that he much desired to make a feast to the Kichi Manito, or Great Spirit, who had preserved himself and his family through the winter, and brought them in safety to the lake. On his receiving my consent, the women went to the spot where we had killed the bear, and where the carcass had been left in safety, buried deep in the snow. They brought the booty back with them, and kettles being hung over the fires, the whole bear was dressed for the feast.

About an hour after dark, accompanied by four of my men, I repaired to the place of sacrifice, according to invitation. The number of the Indians exactly equalled ours, there being two men and three women ; so that together we were ten per-

sons, upon whom it was incumbent to eat up the
whole bear.   I was obliged to receive into my own
plate, or dish, a portion of not less than ten pounds
weight, and each of my men were supplied with
twice this quantity.   As to the Indians, one of
them had to his share the head, the breast, the
heart, with its surrounding fat, and all the four feet;
and the whole of this he swallowed in two hours.
He, as well as the rest, had finished before I had
got through half my toil; and my men were
equally behind-hand. In this situation, one of them
resorted to an experiment which had a ludicrous
issue, and which, at the same time, served to discover a fresh feature in the superstitions of the Indians.   Having first observed to us, that a part of
the cheer would be very acceptable to him the next
day, when his appetite should be returned, he
withdrew a part of the contents of his dish, and
made it fast to the girdle which he wore under his
shirt.   While he disposed in this manner of his su-
perabundance, I, who found myself unable to perform my part, requested the Indians to assist me;
and this they cheerfully did, eating what I had found
too much, with as much apparent ease as if their
stomachs had been previously empty.   The feast
being brought to an end, and the prayer and thanks-
giving pronounced, those near the door departed ; but, when the poor fellow who had concealed
his meat, and who had to pass from the further end
of the lodge, rose up to go, two dogs, guided by

the scent, laid hold of the treasure, and tore it to the ground. The Indians were greatly astonished ; but, presently observed, that the Great Spirit had led the dogs by inspiration to the act, in order to frustrate the profane attempt to steal away this portion of the offering. As matters stood, the course they took was to put the meat into the fire, and there consume it.

On the 20th of April, the ice broke up, and several canoes arrived, filled with women and children, who reported that the men of their band were all gone out to war, against the Nadowessies. On the 15th of May, a part of the warriors, with some others, arrived, in fifty canoes, almost every one of which had a cargo of furs. The warriors gave me some account of their campaign ; stating, that they had set out in search of the enemy, four hundred strong ; and that on the fourth day from their leaving their village, they had met the enemy, and been engaged in battle. The battle, as they related, raged the greater part of the day ; and in the evening, the Nadowessies, to the number of six hundred, fell back, across a river which lay behind them, encamping in this position for the night. The Chipeways had thirty-five killed ; and they took advantage of the suspension of the fray, to *prepare the bodies* of their friends, and then retired to a small distance from the place, expecting the Nadowessies to recross the stream in the morning,

and come again to blows.   In this, however, they
were disappointed ; for the Nadowessies continued
their retreat, without even doing the honours of
war to the slain.   To do these honours is to scalp ;
and to *prepare the bodies* is to dress and paint the
remains of the dead, preparatorily to this mark of
attention from the enemy : " The neglect," said the
Chipeways, " was an affront to us—a disgrace ;
" because we consider it an honour, to have the
" scalps of our countrymen exhibited in the villa-
" ges of our enemies, in testimony of our valour."

The concourse of Indians, already mentioned,
with others who came after, all rich in furs, enabled me very speedily to close my traffic for the
spring, disposing of all the goods, which, on taking
M. Cadotte into partnership, had been left in my own
hands.   I found myself in possession of a hundred
and fifty packs of beaver, weighing a hundred
pounds each, besides twenty-five packs of otter
and marten skins ; and with this part of the fruits
of my adventure, I embarked for Michilimackinac,
sailing in company with fifty canoes of Indians,
who had still a hundred packs of beaver, which I
was unable to purchase.

On my way, I encamped a second time at the
mouth of the Ontonagan, and now took the opportunity of going ten miles up the river, with Indian
guides. The object, which I went most expressly to

see, and to which I had the satisfaction of being led, was a mass of copper, of the weight, according to my estimate, of no less than five ton. Such was its pure and malleable state, that with an axe I was able to cut off a portion, weighing a hundred pounds. On viewing the surrounding surface, I conjectured that the mass, at some period or other, had rolled from the side of a lofty hill, which rises at its back.

CHAPTER III.

Author winters at the Sault de Sainte-Marie.
Scarcity of Provisions. The Man-eater.

I PASSED the winter following at the Sault de
Sainte-Marie. Fish, at this place, are usually so
abundant, in the autumn, that precautions are not
taken for a supply of provisions for the winter; but,
this year the fishery failed, and the early setting-in
of the frost rendered it impracticable to obtain assistance from Michilimackinac. To the increase
of our difficulties, five men, whom, on the prospect
of distress, I had sent to subsist themselves at a distant post, came back, on the day before Christmas-
day, driven in by want.

Under these circumstances, and having heard
that fish might be found in Oak-bay, called by the
French, Anse à la Pêche, or Fishing-cove, which is
on the north side of Lake Superior, at the distance
of twelve leagues from the Sault, I lost no time in
repairing thither, taking with me several men, with
a pint of maize only for each person.

In Oak-bay, we were generally able to obtain a supply of food, sometimes doing so with great facility, but at others going to bed hungry. After being here a fortnight, we were joined by a body of Indians, flying, like ourselves, from famine. Two days after, there came a young Indian out of the woods, alone, and reporting that he had left the family to which he belonged behind, in a starving condition, and unable, from their weakly and exhausted state, to pursue their journey to the bay. The appearance of this youth was frightful ; and from his squalid figure there issued a stench which none of us could support.

His arrival struck our camp with horror and uneasiness ; and it was not long before the Indians came to me, saying, that they suspected he had been eating human flesh, and even that he had killed and devoured the family which he pretended to have left behind.

These charges, upon being questioned, he denied ; but, not without so much equivocation in his answers as to increase the presumption against him. In consequence, the Indians determined on travelling a day's journey, on his track ; observing, that they should be able to discover, from his encampments, whether he were guilty or not. The next day, they returned, bringing with them a human hand and skull. The hand had been left roasting before a fire, while the intestines, taken out of the body from which it was cut, hung fresh upon a neighbouring tree.

The youth, being informed of these discoveries, and further questioned, confessed the crime of which he was accused. From the account he now proceeded to give, it appeared that the family had consisted of his uncle and aunt, their four children and himself. One of the children was a boy of fifteen years of age. His uncle, after firing at several beasts of the chase, all of which he missed, fell into despondence, and persuaded himself that it was the will of the Great Spirit that he should perish. In this state of mind, he requested his wife to kill him. The woman refused to comply; but the two lads, one of them, as has been said, the nephew, and the other the son of the unhappy man, agreed between themselves to murder him, to prevent, as our informant wished us to believe, his murdering them. Accomplishing their detestable purpose, they devoured the body; and famine pressing upon them still closer, they successively killed the three younger children, upon whose flesh they subsisted for some time, and with a part of which the parricides at length set out for the lake, leaving the woman, who was too feeble to travel, to her fate. On their way, their foul victuals failed; the youth before us killed his companion ; and it was a part of the remains of this last victim that had been discovered at the fire.

The Indians entertain an opinion, that the man, who has once made human flesh his food, will never afterward be satisfied with any other. It is probable that we saw things in some measure through the medium of our prejudices ; but, I confess that this distressing object appeared to verify the doctrine. He ate with relish nothing that was given him ; but, indifferent to the food prepared, fixed his eyes continually on the children which were in the Indian lodge, and frequently exclaimed, " How fat they are !"—It was perhaps not unnatural, that after long acquaintance with no human form but such as was gaunt and pale from want of food, a man's eyes should be almost riveted upon any thing, where misery had not made such inroads, and still more upon the bloom and plumpness of childhood ; and the exclamation might be the most innocent, and might proceed from an involuntary and unconquerable sentiment of admiration.—Be this as it may, his behaviour was considered, and not less naturally, as marked with the most alarming symptoms ; and the Indians, apprehensive that he would prey upon their children, resolved on putting him to death. They did this the next day, with a single stroke of an axe, aimed at his head from behind, and of the

27

approach of which he had not the smallest intimation.

Soon after this affair, our supply of fish, even here, began to fail; and we resolved, in consequence, to return to the Sault, in the hope that some supply might have arrived there. Want, however, still prevailed at that place, and no stranger had visited it : we set off, therefore, to Michilimackinac, taking with us only one meal's provision, for each person. Happily, at our first encampment, an hour's fishing procured us seven trout, each of from ten pounds weight to twenty. At the river Miscoutinsaki, we found two lodges of Indians, who had fish, and who generously gave us part. The next day, we continued our journey, till, meeting with a *caribou*, I was so fortunate as to kill it. We encamped close to the carcass, which weighed about four hundred pounds, and subsisted ourselves upon it for two days. On the seventh day of our march, we reached Fort Michilimackinac, where our difficulties ended.

On the 1st of July, there arrived a hundred canoes from the north-west, laden with beaver.

CHAPTER IV.

THE same year, I chose my wintering-ground at Michipicoten, on the north side of Lake Superior, distant fifty leagues from the Sault de Sainte-Marie. On my voyage, after passing the great capes which are at the mouth of the lake, I observed the banks to be low and stony, and in some places running a league back, to the feet of a ridge of mountains.

At Point Mamance, the beach appeared to abound in mineral substances ; and I met with a vein of lead-ore, where the metal abounded in the form of cubical crystals. Still coasting along the lake, I found several veins of copper-ore, of that kind which the miners call gray ore.

From Mamance to Nanibojou is fifteen leagues. Nanibojou is on the eastern side of the Bay of Michipicoten. At the opposite point, or cape, are several small islands, under one of which, according to Indian tradition, is buried Nanibojou, a person of the most sacred memory. Nanibojou, is otherwise called by the names of Minabojou, Michabou, Messou, Shactac, and a variety of others, but of all of which the interpretation appears to be, *The Great Hare.* The traditions, related of the Great Hare, are as varied as his name. He was represented to me as the founder, and indeed creator, of the Indian nations of North-America. He lived originally toward the going down of the sun, where being warned, in a dream, that the inhabitants would be drowned by a general flood, produced by heavy rains, he built a raft, on which he afterward preserved his own family, and all the animal world without exception. According to his dream, the rains fell, and a flood ensued. His raft drifted for many moons, during which no land was discovered. His family began to despair of a termination to the calamity; and the animals, who had then the use of speech, mur-

mured loudly against him.   In the end, he produced a new earth, placed the animals upon it, and
created man.

At a subsequent period, he took from the animals the use of speech.   This act of severity was
performed in consequence of a conspiracy, into
which they had entered against the human race.   At
the head of the conspiracy was the bear ; and the
great increase, which had taken place among the
animals, rendered their numbers formidable.—I
have heard many other stories concerning Nanibojou, and many have been already given to the
public ; and this at least is certain, that sacrifices
are offered, on the island which is called his grave
or tumulus, by all who pass it.   I landed there, and
found on the projecting rocks a quantity of tobacco,
rotting in the rain ; together with kettles, broken
guns and a variety of other articles.   His spirit is
supposed to make this its constant residence ; and
here to preside over the lake, and over the Indians,
in their navigation and fishing.

This island lies no further from the main, than
the distance of five hundred yards.   On the opposite beach, I found several pieces of virgin copper,
of which many were remarkable for their form ;
some resembling leaves of vegetables, and others

animals.   Their weight was from an ounce to three pounds.

From the island to my proposed wintering-ground, the voyage was about ten leagues. The lake is here bordered by a rugged and elevated country, consisting in mountains, of which, for the most part, the feet are in the water, and the heads in the clouds. The river which falls into the bay is a large one, but has a bar at its entrance, over which there is no more than four feet water.

On reaching the trading-post, which was an old one of French establishment, I found ten lodges of Indians. These were *Gens de Terres*, or *O'pimittish Ininiwac*, of which nation I have already had occasion to speak.* It is scattered over all the country between the Gulf of Saint-Lawrence and Lake Arabuthcow, and between Lake Superior and Hudson's Bay. Its language is a mixture of those of its neighbours, the Chipeways and Cristinaux.† The men and women wear their hair in the same fashion ; and are otherwise so much dressed alike, that it is often difficult to dis-

---

* See Part I. Chapter 6. They are also called *Tetes de Boule.*

† The same with Kinistinaux, Killistinoes, Criqs, Cris, Crees, &c. &c. &c.

tinguish the sexes. Their lodges, on the insuffi-
ciency of which I have before remarked, have no
covering, except the branches of the spruce-fir;
and these habitations, as well as the clothes and persons of the inhabitants, are full of dirt and vermin.
Such is the inhospitality of the country over which
they wander, that only a single family can live
together in the winter season; and this sometimes
seeks subsistence in vain, on an area of five hundred square miles. They can stay in one place
only till they have destroyed all its hares; and
when these fail, they have no resource but in the
leaves and shoots of trees, or in defect of these, in
cannibalism. Most of these particulars, however,
are to be regarded as strong traits, by which the
sorrows and calamities of the country admit of being characterized, rather than as parts of an accurate
delineation of its more ordinary state.

Among such of these Indians as I knew, one of
them was married to his own daughter, who had
brought him several children; and I was told by
his companions, that it was common among them
for a man to have at the same time, both a mother
and her daughter for wives.

To the ten lodges, I advanced goods to a large
amount, allowing every man credit for a hundred beaver-skins, and every woman for thirty. In
this, I went beyond what I had done for the Chipe-

ways, a proceeding to which I was emboldened by
the high character, for honesty, which is supported
by this otherwise abject people. Within a few days
after their departure, others arrived; and by the
fifteenth of October, I had seen, or so I was informed, all the Indians of this quarter, and which
belong to a thousand square miles. They were
comprised in no more than eighteen families; and
even these, in summer, could not find food in
the country, were it not for the fish in the streams
and lakes.

The country, immediately contiguous to my wintering-ground, was mountainous in every direction; and the mountains were separated from each
other rather by lakes than valleys, the quantity of
water every where exceeding that of the land. On
the summits of some of the mountains there were
sugar-maple trees; but, with these exceptions, the
uplands had no other growth than spruce-firs and
pines, nor the lowlands than birch and poplar.
Occasionally, I saw a few *cariboux;* and hares and
partridges supplied my Sundays' dinners.—By
Christmas-day, the lake was covered with ice.

CHAPTER V.

Maple-sugar making. Depth of Snow. Wild-fowl—short-lived abundance. Indians bring in their Skins. Author passes a second Winter at Michipicoten—sails for the Sault de Sainte-Marie. Storm at the Island of Nanibojou. Famine. Canadians propose to kill and eat a Young Woman. Tripe de Roche—nutritive quality of that vegetable. Arrival at the Sault and return to Michipicoten.

IN the beginning of April, I prepared to make maple-sugar, building for this purpose a house, in a hollow dug out of the snow, The house was seven feet high, but yet was lower than the snow.

On the twenty-fourth, I began my manufacture. On the twenty-eighth, the lands below were covered with a thick fog. All was calm, and from the top of the mountain not a cloud was to be discovered in the horizon. Descending the next day, I found half a foot of new-fallen snow, and learned that it had blown hard in the valleys the day before ; so

28

that I perceived I had been making sugar in a region above the clouds.

Sugar-making continued till the twelfth of May.
On the mountain, we eat nothing but our sugar,
during the whole period. Each man consumed a
pound a day, desired no other food, and was visibly
nourished by it.

After returning to the banks of the river, wild-
fowl appeared in such abundance that a day's subsistence, for fifty men, could without difficulty be
shot daily by one ; but, all this was the affair of less
than a week, before the end of which the water,
which had been covered, was left naked ; and the
birds had fled away to the northward.

On the twentieth day of the month, the first
party of Indians came in from their winter's hunt.
During the season, some of them had visited one
of the factories of the Hudson's Bay Company.
Within a few days following, I had the satisfaction of seeing all those to whom I had advanced
goods return. Out of two thousand skins, which
was the amount of my outstanding debts, not
thirty remained unpaid ; and even the trivial
loss, which I did suffer, was occasioned by the
death of one of the Indians, for whom his family brought, as they said, all the skins of which
he died possessed, and offered to pay the rest from

among themselves:—his manes, they observed, would not be able to enjoy peace, while his name remained in my books, and his debts were left unsatisfied.

In the spring, at Michilimackinac, I met with a Mr. Alexander Baxter, recently arrived from England, on report of the ores existing in this country. To this gentleman, I communicated my mineralogical observations and specimens, collected both on my voyages and at my wintering-ground; and I was thus introduced into a partnership, which was soon afterward formed, for working the mines of Lake Superior.

Meanwhile, I prepared to pass a second winter at Michipicoten, which I reached at the usual season. In the month of October, all the Indians being supplied, and at the chase, I resolved on indulging myself in a voyage to the Sault de Sainte-Marie, and took with me three Canadians, and a young Indian woman, who wished to see her relations there. As the distance was short, and we were to fish by the way, we took no other provision than a quart of maize for each person.

On the first night, we encamped on the island of Nanibojou, and set our net. We certainly neglected the customary offerings, and an Indian would not fail to attribute it to this cause, that in the night there arose a violent storm, which continued for three days, in which it was impossible for us to visit our net. In consequence, we subsisted ourselves on our maize, the whole of which we nearly finished. On the evening of the third day, the storm abated, and we hastened to examine the net. It was gone. To return to Michipicoten was impossible, the wind being ahead ; and we steered therefore for the Sault. But, in the evening, the wind came round, and blew a gale all that night, and for the nine following days. During all this time, the waves were so high, and broke so violently on the beach, that a canoe could not be put into the water.

When we first disembarked, we had not enough maize to afford a single day's provision for our party, consisting, as it did, of five persons. What there was, we consumed on the first evening, reckoning upon a prosperous voyage the next morning. On the first and second days, I went out to hunt ; but, after ranging for many miles among the mountains, I returned, in both instances without success. On the third day, I found myself too weak to walk many yards without stopping to rest myself ; and I returned in the evening with no more than two snow-birds.*

* Emberiza hyemalis.

On my arrival, one of my men informed me, that the other two had proposed to kill and feed upon the young woman ; and, on my examining them as to the truth of this accusation, they freely avowed it, and seemed to be much dissatisfied at my opposition to their scheme.

The next morning, I ascended a lofty mountain, on the top of which I found a very high rock, and this covered with a lichen, which the Chipeways call *waac*, and the Canadians, *tripe de roche*. I had previously been informed, that on occasions of famine, this vegetable has often been resorted to for food. No sooner, therefore, had I discovered it, than I began to descend the mountain, to fetch the men and the Indian woman. The woman was well acquainted with the mode of preparing the lichen for the stomach, which is done by boiling it down into a mucilage, as thick as the white of an egg. In a short time, we obtained a hearty meal; for though our food was of a bitter and disagreeable taste, we felt too much joy in finding it, and too much relief in eating it, not to partake of it with appetite and pleasure. As to the rest, it saved the life of the poor woman; for the men, who had projected to kill her, would unquestionably have accomplished their purpose. One of them gave me to understand, that he was not absolutely a novice in such an affair ; that he had wintered in the northwest, and had been obliged tò eat human flesh.

On the evening of the ninth day, the wind fell, and our canoe was launched, though not without difficulty, from the weakly state of the crew. We paddled all night, but continually fell asleep; and whenever my own eyes were closed, I dreamed of tempting food.

The next morning, we discovered two canoes of Indians, on their way from the Sault. On informing them of our condition, they supplied us with as many fish as we were willing to accept; and no sooner were we possessed of this treasure, than we put ashore, made a fire, and refreshed ourselves with a plentiful breakfast. At night, we reached the Sault. Our change of diet had very serious effects upon our health; so that, for myself, I had nearly fallen a victim: but, after a few days, we recovered, and returned safely to Michipicoten.

CHAPTER VI.

Ile de Maurepas. Island of Yellow Sands. Fables and Traditions. Attempt to cultivate a Garden at Michipicoten. Mine-Company of Lake Superior established.

IN the spring of 1769, as soon as the lake was cleared of ice, I embarked with two Indians, to visit the Island of Michipicoten, or Ile de Maurepas, distant ten leagues. As we approached it, it appeared large and mountainous. The Indians had informed me, that it contained shining rocks, and stones of rare description. I found it one solid rock, thinly covered with soil, except in the valleys; but generally well wooded. Its circumference is twelve leagues. On examining the surface, I saw nothing remarkable, except large veins of transparent spar, and a mass of rock, at the south end of the island, which appeared to be composed of iron-ore.

Disappointed in my expectations here, my curiosity was raised anew, by the account given me by my companions, of another island, almost as

large as that on which I was, and lying a little further to the southward. This they described as
covered with a heavy yellow sand, which I was
credulous enough to fancy must be gold. All they
knew, however, of the island and its heavy yellow
sand, was from the report of some of their ancestors, concerning whom a tradition had come down
to them, that being blown upon the former by a
storm, they had escaped with difficulty from the
enormous snakes by which it is inhabited, and
which are the guardians of the yellow sand.* I was

* Captain Carver, who visited Lake Superior about the
year 1766, learned something of the fables of the yellow
sand, though he places the treasure upon the Ile de Maurepas, and falls into other errors. His observations are as
follow :—" There are many islands in this lake, two of
" which are very large ; and if the land of them is proper
" for cultivation, there appears to be sufficient to form on
" each a considerable province ; especially on Ile Royale,
" which cannot be less than a hundred miles long, and in
" many places forty broad. But, there is no way at present
" of ascertaining the exact length or breadth of either.
" Even the French, who always kept a small schooner on
" this lake, whilst they were in possession of Canada, by
" which they could have made this discovery, have only ac-
" quired a slight knowledge of the external parts of these
" islands : at least, they have never published any account
" of the internal parts of them, that I could get intelli-
" gence of.

eager to visit so remarkable a spot, and being told
that in clear weather it was visible from the south-

" Nor was I able to discover, from any of the conversa-
" tions which I had with the neighbouring Indians, that
" they had ever made any settlements on them, or even
" landed there, on their hunting excursions. From what
" I could gather by their discourse, they suppose them to
" have been, from the first formation, the residence of the
" Great Spirit ; and relate many magical tricks, that had
" been experienced by such as were obliged through stress
" of weather to take shelter on them.

" One of the Chipeways told me, that some of their
" people were once driven on the Island de Maurepas,
" which lies to the north-east part of the lake, and found on
" it large quantities of heavy, shining yellow sand, that from
" their description must have been gold-dust. Being struck
" with the beautiful appearance of it, in the morning, when
" they re-entered their canoe, they attempted to bring some
" away ; but, a spirit of amazing size, according to their
" account, sixty feet in height, strode into the water, after
" them, and commanded them to deliver back what they
" had taken away. Terrified at his gigantic stature, and
" seeing that he had nearly overtaken them, they were glad
" to restore their shining treasure ; on which they were suf-
" fered to depart without further molestation. Since this
" incident, no Indian, that has ever heard of it, will venture
" near the same haunted coast. Besides this, they recounted
" to me many other stories of these islands, equally fabu-
" lous."—*Three Years' Travels through the Interior Parts
of North America, &c. By Captain Jonathan Carver, of the
Provincial Troops, &c.*

ward of the Ile de Maurepas, I waited there two days ; but, the weather continuing hazy, I returned unsatisfied to my post.

This year, I attempted to cultivate culinary vegetables at Michipicoten ; but without success. It was not at this time believed, that the potatoe could thrive at Michilimackinac. At Michipicoten, the small quantity of this root which I raised was destroyed by the frost, in the ensuing winter.

In 1770, Mr. Baxter, who had sailed for England, returned, bringing with him papers, by which, with Mr. Bostwick and himself, I was constituted a joint-agent and partner, in and for a company of adventurers for working the mines of Lake Superior. We passed the winter together at the Sault de Sainte-Marie, and built a barge, fit for the navigation of the lake ; at the same time laying the keel of a sloop of forty tons. Early in May, 1771, the lake becoming navigable, we departed from Point aux Pins, our ship-yard, at which there is a safe harbour, and of which the distance from the Sault is three leagues. We sailed for the Island of Yellow Sands, promising ourselves to make our fortunes, in defiance of its serpents.

CHAPTER VII.

Visit the Island of Yellow Sands. Operations of the Mine-Company—its dissolution.

AFTER a search of two days, we discovered the island with our glass ; and on the third morning, the weather being fair, steered for it at an early hour. At two o'clock in the afternoon, we disembarked upon the beach.

I was the first to land, carrying with me my loaded gun, and resolved to meet with courage the guardians of the gold. But, as we had not happened to run our barge upon the yellow sands in the first instance, so no immediate attack was to be feared. A wood was before us, at some little distance from the water's edge ; and I presently discovered the tracks of *cariboux*.

Soon after I entered the woods, three of these animals discovered themselves, and turning round, gazed at me with much apparent surprise. I fired at one of them and killed it ; and at a mile further I killed a second. Their size was equal to that of a three-year old heifer. The day following, I killed three.

The island is much smaller than I had been led to suppose it ; its circumference not exceeding twelve miles. It is very low, and contains many small lakes. These latter I conjecture to have been produced by the damming up of the streams by beaver. though those animals must have left the island, or perished, after destroying the wood. The only high land is toward the east.

A stay of three days did not enable us to find gold, nor even the yellow sands. At the same time, no serpents appeared, to terrify us ; not even the smallest and most harmless snake. But, to support the romance, it might be inferred, that the same agency which hid the one had changed the other ; and why should not the magic of the place display itself in a thousand varied exhibitions ? Why should not the serpents have been transformed into hawks ? and why should not the demons delight in belying every succeeding visitor, by never showing the same objects twice? Sure I am, that the hawks abounded when we were there. They hovered round us, and appeared even angry at our intrusion, pecking at us, and keeping us in continual alarm for our faces. One of them actually took my cap from off my head.

On one of the lakes, we saw geese; and there were a few pigeons. The only four-footed animal was the *caribou*, and this, it is probable, was first conveyed to the island on some mass of drifting ice. It was however no new inhabitant; for, in numerous instances, I found the bones of *cariboux*, apparently in entire skeletons, with only the tops of their horns projecting from the surface, while moss or vegetable earth concealed the rest. Skeletons were so frequent, as to suggest a belief, that want of food, in this confined situation, had been the destruction of many; nor is any thing more probable: and yet the absence of beasts of prey might be the real cause. In forests more ordinarily circumstanced, the graminivorous animals must usually fall a prey to the carnivorous, long before the arrival of old age; but, in an asylum such as this, they may await the decay of nature.

The alarm of these animals, during our stay, was manifested in the strongest manner. At our first arrival, they discovered mere surprise, running off to a distance, and then returning, as if out of curiosity to examine the strangers. Soon, however, they discovered us to be dangerous visitors, and then took to running from one place to another, in confusion. In the three days of our stay, we killed thirteen.

The island is distant sixty miles from the north shore of Lake Superior. There is no land visible to the south of it, except a small island, on which we landed.*

On the fourth day, after drying our *cariboux-meat*, we sailed for Nanibojou, which we reached in eighteen hours, with a fair breeze. On the next day, the miners examined the coast of Nanibojou, and found several veins of copper and lead; and after this returned to Point aux Pins, where we erected an air-furnace. The assayer made a report on the ores which we had collected, stating that the lead-ore contained silver in the proportion of forty ounces to a ton; but, the copper-ore, only in very small proportion indeed.

From Point aux Pins, we crossed to the south side of the lake, and encamped on Point aux Iroquois.

Mr. Norburg, a Russian gentleman, acquainted with metals, and holding a commission in the sixtieth regiment, and then in garrison at Michilimackinac, accompanied us on this latter expedition. As we rambled, examining the *shods*, or loose

---

* The reader is not to look into any gazetteer for the *Island of Yellow Sands*. It is perhaps that which the French denominated, the Ile de Pontchartrain.

stones, in search of minerals, Mr. Norburg chanced to meet with one, of eight pounds weight, of a blue colour, and semi-transparent. This he carried to England, where it produced in the proportion of sixty pounds of silver to a hundred weight of ore. It was reposited in the British Museum. The same Mr. Norburg was shortly afterward appointed to the government of Lake George, in the province of New-York.

Hence, we coasted westward; but found nothing till we reached the Ontonagan, where, besides the detached masses of copper, formerly mentioned, we saw much of the same metal bedded in stone. Proposing to ourselves to make a trial on the hill, till we were better able to go to work upon the solid rock, we built a house, and sent to the Sault de Sainte-Marie for provisions. At the spot, pitched upon for the commencement of our preparations, a green-coloured water, which tinged iron of a copper-colour, issued from the hill; and this the miners called a *leader*. In digging, they found frequent masses of copper, some of which were of three pounds weight. Having arranged every thing for the accommodation of the miners during the winter, we returned to the Sault.

Early in the spring of 1772, we sent a boat-load of provisions; but, it came back on the twentieth day of June, bringing with it, to our surprise, the whole establishment of miners. They reported, that in the course of the winter they had penetrated forty feet into the hill ; but, that on the arrival of the thaw, the clay, on which, on account of its stiffness, they had relied, and neglected to secure it by supporters, had fallen in : that to recommence their search would be attended with much labour and cost ; that from the detached masses of metal, which to the last had daily presented themselves, they supposed there might be ultimately reached some body of the same, but could form no conjecture of its distance, except that it was probably so far off as not to be pursued without sinking an air-shaft : and, lastly, that this work would require the hands of more men than could be fed, in the actual situation of the country.

Here our operations in this quarter ended. The metal was probably within our reach ; but, if we had found it, the expense of carrying it to Montréal must have exceeded its marketable value. It was never for the exportation of copper that our company was formed ; but, always with a view to the silver which it was hoped the ores, whether of copper or lead, might in sufficient quantity contain. The copper-ores of Lake Superior can never be profitably sought for but for local consumption. The country must be cultivated and peopled, be-

fore they can deserve notice.＊   The neighbouring
lands are good.   I distributed seed-maize among

＊ The copper-mines of Lake Superior have been more
than once represented to the world in colours capable of de-
ceiving fresh adventurers; and the statement in the text will
not have been uselessly made, if it should at any time serve as
a beacon to the unwary.   The author of Voyages from Montreal, &c. has recently observed, that the " Americans, soon
" after they got possession of the country, sent an engineer;"
and that he " should not be surprised to hear of their employ-
" ing people to work the mine.. Indeed," he adds, " it
" might be well worthy the attention of the British subjects
" to work the mines on the north coast, though they are not
" supposed to be so rich as those on the south;"—and Captain
Carver has given the following account of the identical undertaking above described: " A company of adventurers from
" England began, soon after the conquest of Canada, to bring
" away some of this metal; *but the distracted situation of*
" *affairs in America has obliged them to relinquish their scheme.*
" It might in future times be made a very advantageous
" trade; as the metal, which *costs nothing* on the spot, and
" requires but little expense to get it on board, could be con-
" veyed in boats or canoes through the Falls of Sainte-Marie,
" to the Isle of Saint-Joseph, which lies at the bottom of the
" strait, near the entrance into Lake Huron; from thence it
" might be put on board larger vessels, and in them transport-
" ed across that lake, to the Falls of Niagara; then being car-
" ried by land, across the *portage*, it might be conveyed with-
" out much more obstruction to Quebec.   The cheapness
" and ease with which any quantity of it may be procured,
" will make up for the length of way that is necessary to
" transport it, before it reaches the sea-coast; and enable the

the Indians here, which they planted accordingly. They did the same the following year, and in both instances had good crops. Whether or not they continued the practice, I cannot say. There might be much danger of their losing the seed; for their way was, to eat the maize green, and save only a small quantity for sowing.

In the following month of August, we launched our sloop, and carried the miners to the vein of copper-ore on the north side of the lake. Little was done during the winter; but, by dint of labour, performed between the commencement of the spring of 1773, and the ensuing month of September, they penetrated thirty feet into the solid rock. The rock was blasted with great difficulty; and the vein, which, at the beginning, was of the breadth of four feet, had in the progress contracted into four inches. Under these circumstances, we desisted, and carried the miners back to the Sault. What copper-ore we had collected, we sent to England; but, the next season, we were informed, that the partners there declined entering into further expenses.—In the interim, we had carried the miners along the north shore, as far as the river Pic, making, however, no discovery of

" proprietors to send it to foreign markets on as good terms as " it can be exported from other countries."—*Three Years' Travels, &c.*

importance. This year, therefore, 1774, Mr. Baxter disposed of the sloop, and other effects of the Company, and paid its debts.

The partners, in England, were His Royal Highness the Duke of Gloucester, Mr. Secretary Townshend, Sir Samuel Tutchet, Baronet; Mr. Baxter, consul of the empress of Russia; and Mr. Cruickshank : in America, Sir William Johnson, Baronet; Mr. Bostwick, Mr. Baxter and myself.

A charter had been petitioned for, and obtained; but, owing to our ill success, it was never taken from the seal-office.

CHAPTER VIII.

PENDING this enterprise, I had still pursued
the Indian trade ; 'and on its failure I applied myself to that employment with more assiduity than
ever, and resolved on visiting the countries to the
north-west of Lake Superior.

On the 10th day of June, 1775, I left the Sault,
with goods and provisions to the value of three
thousand pounds sterling, on board twelve small
canoes, and four larger ones. The provisions made

the chief bulk of the cargo; no further supply being obtainable, till we should have advanced far
into the country. Each small canoe was navigated
by three men, and each larger one by four.

On the 20th, we passed the Tête de la Loutre, or
Otter's Head, so named from a rock, of about thirty
feet in height, and fifteen in circumference, and which
stands vertically, as if raised by the hand of man.
What increases the appearance of art, is a hollow
in the adjacent mass of rock, which its removal
might be thought to have left. In the evening, we
encamped at the mouth of the Pijitic, a river as large
as that of Michipicoten, and which in like manner
takes its rise in the high lands lying between
Lake Superior and Hudson's Bay. From Michipicoten to the Pijitic, the coast of the lake is mountainous: the mountains are covered with pine, and
the valleys with spruce-fir.

It was by the river Pijitic* that the French ascended in 1750, when they plundered one of the
factories in Hudson's Bay, and carried off the two
small pieces of brass cannon which fell again into

* According to Carver, it was by the Michipicoten. If
he is correct, it must have been from Moose Fort, in
James's Bay, and not from Fort Churchill, that they took
the cannon.

the hands of the English at Michilimackinac. On the river are a band of Wood Indians, who are sometimes troublesome to the traders passing.

On the 21st, I left the Pijitic, and crossing a bay, three leagues in breadth, landed on Pic Island. From Pic Island, I coasted ten leagues, and then encamped on an island opposite the Pays Plat, or Flat Country, a name borrowed from the Indians, and occasioned by the shoal-water which here extends far into the lake, and by the flat and low lands which lie between the water and the mountains.

The Pays Plat is intersected by several large rivers, and particularly the Nipigon, so called after Lake Nipigon, of which it is the discharge. By this river, the French carried on a considerable trade with the Northern Indians. They had a fort or trading-house at its mouth, and annually drew from it a hundred packs of beaver, of a quality more in esteem than that from the north-west. They had another trading-house at Caministiquia. —As we proceed north-west along the lake, the mountains recede widely from the beach.

On the 24th, I left the northern shore, and in four days reached the Grand Portage. The intervening islands consist almost entirely in rock. The largest, called Ile au Tonnerre, or Thunder

Island, is said, by the Indians, to be peculiarly subject to thunder-storms.   At the Grand Portage, I
found the traders in a state of extreme reciprocal
hostility, each pursuing his interests in such a manner as might most injure his neighbour.   The consequences were very hurtful to the morals of the
Indians.

The transportation of the goods at this *grand
portage*, or *great carrying-place*, was a work of
seven days of severe and dangerous exertion, at
the end of which we encamped on the river Aux
Groseilles.*   The Grand Portage consists in two
ridges of land, between which is a deep glen or
valley, with good meadow-lands, and a broad stream
of water.   The lowlands are covered chiefly with
birch and poplar, and the high with pine.   I was
now in what is technically called the *north-west ;*
that is, the country north-west of Lake Superior.
The canoes here employed are smaller than those
which are used between Montréal and Michilimackinac, and in Lake Superior ; being only four
fathom and a half in length.   It is the duty of the
head and stern men to carry the canoe.   I engaged
two of these to winter with me, at the wages of four

* The same with what a recent traveller describes as the
" river du Tourt," (Tourtre,)—" Dove or Pigeon river."

hundred dollars each, and an equipment of the value, at the Grand Portage, of one hundred more.

On the eighth, we ascended the Groseilles, to the carrying-place called the Portage du Perdrix, where the river falls down a precipice of the height of a hundred feet. At the place, where, after passing the Grand Portage, we first launched our canoes on the Groseilles, the stream is thirty yards wide. From this spot, it proceeds, with numerous falls, to Lake Superior, which it enters about six leagues to the northward of the Grand Portage.

Next day, at the Portage aux Outardes, we left the Groseilles, and carrying our canoes and merchandise for three miles, over a mountain, came at length to a small lake. This was the beginning of a chain of lakes, extending for fifteen leagues, and separated by carrying-places of from half a mile to three miles in length. At the end of this chain, we reached the heads of small streams which flow to the north-westward. The region of the lakes is called the Hauteur de Terre, or *Land's Height*. It is an elevated tract of country, not inclining in any direction, and diversified on its surface with small hills. The wood is abundant ; but consists principally in birch, pine, spruce-fir and a small quantity of maple.

By the twelfth, we arrived where the streams were large enough to float the canoes, with their lading, though the men walked in the water, pushing them along. Next day, we found them sufficiently navigable, though interrupted by frequent falls and carrying-places. On the twentieth, we reached Lake Sagunac, or Saginaga, distant sixty leagues from the Grand Portage. This was the hither-most post in the north-west, established by the French ; and there was formerly a large village of Chipeways here, now destroyed by the Na-dowessies. I found only three lodges, filled with poor, dirty and almost naked inhabitants, of whom I bought fish and wild rice,* which latter they had in great abundance. When populous, this village used to be troublesome to the traders, obstructing their voyages, and extorting liquor and other articles. Lake Sagunac is eight leagues in length by four in breadth. The lands, which are every where covered with spruce, are hilly on the south-west ; but, on the north-east more level. My men were by this time almost exhausted with fatigue ; but, the chief part of the labour was fortunately past.

We now entered Lake à la Pluie, which is fifteen leagues long, by five broad. Its banks are covered with maple and birch. Our encampment was at

---

* Folle avoine, avena fatua, zizania aquatica.

the mouth of the lake, where there is a fall of water
of forty feet, called the Chute de la Chaudière.
The carrying-place is two hundred yards in length.
On the next evening, we encamped at Les Four-
ches, on the River à la Pluie, where there was a
village of Chipeways, of fifty lodges, of whom I
bought new canoes. They insisted further on
having goods given to them on credit, as well as on
receiving some presents. The latter they regarded
as an established tribute, paid them on account of
the ability which they possessed, to put a stop to
all trade with the interior. I gave them rum, with
which they became drunk and troublesome ; and
in the night I left them.

The River à la Pluie is forty leagues long, of a
gentle current, and broken only by one rapid. Its
banks are level to a great distance, and composed
of a fine soil, which was covered with luxuriant
grass. They were perfect solitudes, not even a
canoe presenting itself, along my whole navigation
of the stream. I was greatly struck with the beauty
of the scene, as well as with its fitness for agricul-
tural settlements, in which provisions might be
raised for the north-west.

On the thirtieth, we reached the Lake of the
Woods, or Lake des Iles, at the entrance of which
was an Indian village, of a hundred souls, where we

obtained a further supply of fish. Fish appeared to
be the summer food.

From this village, we received ceremonious presents.   The mode with the Indians is, first to collect all the provisions they can spare, and place
them in a heap ; after which they send for the trader, and address him in a formal speech.   They
tell him, that the Indians are happy in seeing him
return into their country ; that they have been long
in expectation of his arrival ; that their wives have
deprived themselves of their provisions, in order to
afford him a supply ; that they are in great want,
being destitute of every thing, and particularly
of ammunition and clothing ; and that what they
most long for, is a taste of his rum, which they uniformly denominate *milk*.

The present, in return, consisted in one keg of
gunpowder, of sixty pounds weight; a bag of shot,
and another of powder, of eighty pounds each ; a
few smaller articles, and a keg of rum.   The last
appeared to be the chief treasure, though on the
former depended the greater part of their winter's
subsistence.

In a short time, the men began to drink, while
the women brought me a further and very valuable
present, of twenty bags of rice.   This I returned
with goods and rum, and at the same time offered

more, for an additional quantity of rice. A trade
was opened, the women bartering rice, while
the men were drinking. Before morning, I had
purchased a hundred bags, of nearly a bushel measure each. Without a large quantity of rice, the
voyage could not have been prosecuted to its com-
pletion. The canoes, as I have already observed,
are not large enough to carry provisions, leaving
merchandise wholly out of the question.—The
rice grows in shoal water, and the Indians gather it
by shaking the ears into their canoes.

When morning arrived, all the village was
inebriated ; and the danger of misunderstanding
was increased by the facility with which the
women abandoned themselves to my Canadians.
In consequence, I lost no time in leaving the
place.

On the first day of August, we encamped on a
sandy island in the Lake of the Woods, where we
were visited by several canoes, of whom we purchased wild rice. On the fourth, we reached the
Portage du Rat.

The Lake of the Woods is thirty-six leagues
long. On the west side is an old French fort or
trading-house, formerly frequented by numerous
bands of Chipeways, but these have since been
almost entirely destroyed by the Nadowessies.

When strong, they were troublesome. On account of a particular instance of pillage, they have been called *Pilleurs*. The pelican is numerous on this lake. One, which we shot, agreed entirely with the description of M. de Buffon.

On the fifth, we passed the Portage du Rat, which is formed by a rock of about twenty yards long. Here, we met several canoes of Indians, who all begged for rum ; but, they were known to belong to the band of *Pilleurs*, also called the *rogues*, and were on that account refused.

From the Portage du Rat, we descended the great river Winipegon, which is there from one mile to two in breadth, and at every league grows broader. The channel is deep, but obstructed by many islands, of which some are large. For several miles, the stream is confined between perpendicular rocks. The current is strong, and the navigation singularly difficult. Within the space of fifteen leagues, there are seven falls, of from fifty feet to a hundred in height. At sixty leagues from our entrance of the Winipegon, we crossed a carrying-place into the Pinawac ; below which, the dangers of the Winipegon are still further increased. The adjacent lands are mountainous and rocky ; but, some of the high hills are well covered with birch and maple.

The stream of the Pinawa is shallow, and its bed rocky and broken.   The carrying-places are eight in number.   The mosquitoes were here in such clouds as to prevent us from taking aim at the ducks, of which we might else have shot many.

On the thirteenth, we encamped at the Carrying-place of the Lost Child.   Here is a chasm in the rock, no where more than two yards in breadth, but of great and immeasurable depth.   The Indians relate, that many ages past, a child fell into this chasm, from the bottom of which it is still heard, at times, to cry.   In all the wet lands, wild rice grows plentifully.

The Pinawa is twenty leagues long, and discharges itself into Lake du Bonnet,* at three leagues to the north of the mouth of the Winipegon, which falls into the same lake, or rather forms it; for Lake du Bonnet is only a broadened part of the channel of the Winipegon. The lake is two leagues broad; and the river, in its course below, continues broader than it is above, with many islands and deep falls: the danger of the navigation, however, is lessened.

On the sixteenth, we reached Lake Winipegon, at the entrance of which is a large village of Christinaux, a nation which I had not previously seen.

* Cap Lake, in some maps written *Cat Lake*.

The name is variously written ; as, Cristinaux, Kinistineaux, Killistinoes and Killistinaux. Lake Winipegon is sometimes called the Lake of the Killistinons, or Cristinaux. The dress and other exterior appearances of the Cristinaux are very distinguishable from those of the Chipeways and the Wood Indians.

The men were almost entirely naked, and their bodies painted with a red ochre, procured in the mountains, and often called *vermilion*. Every man and boy had his bow strung and in his hand, and his arrow ready, to attack in case of need. Their heads were shaved, or the hair plucked out, all over, except a spot on the crown, of the diameter of a dollar. On this spot, the hair grew long, and was rolled and gathered into a tuft ; and the tuft, which is an object of the greatest care was covered with a piece of skin. The ears were pierced, and filled with the bones of fish and of land animals.—Such was the costume of the young men ; but, among the old, some let their hair grow on all parts of their head, without any seeming regard.

The women wear their hair of a great length, both behind and before, dividing it on the forehead and at the back of the head, and collecting the hair of each side into a roll, which is fastened above the ear ; and this roll, like the tuft on the heads of the men, is covered with a piece of skin. The skin is

painted, or else ornamented with beads of various
colours. The rolls, with their coverings, resemble
a pair of large horns. The ears of the women are
pierced and decorated, like those of the men.

Their clothing is of leather, or dressed skins of
the wild ox and the elk. The dress, falling from the
shoulders to below the knee, is of one entire piece.
Girls of an early age wear their dresses shorter than
those more advanced. The same garment covers
the shoulders and the bosom ; and is fastened by
a strap which passes over the shoulders : it is confined about the waist by a girdle. The stockings
are of leather, made in the fashion of *leggings.*
The arms, to the shoulders, are left naked, or are
provided with sleeves, which are sometimes put
on, and sometimes suffered to hang vacant
from the shoulders. The wrists are adorned
with. bracelets of. copper or brass, manufactured
from old kettles. In general, one person is worth
but one dress ; and this is worn as long as it will
last, or till a new one is made, and then thrown
away.

The women, like the men, paint their faces
with red ochre ; and in addition usually tatoo two
lines, reaching from the lip to the chin, or from the
corners of the mouth to the ears. They omit no
thing to make themselves lovely.

Meanwhile, a favourite employment is that of waging war with certain animals which are in abundance on their persons, and which, as they catch, they eat.   To frequent inquiries, as to the motive for eating them, I was always answered, that they afforded a medicinal food, and great preventive of diseases.

Such are the exterior beauties of the female Cristinaux ; and, not content with the power belonging to these attractions, they condescend to beguile, with gentle looks, the hearts of passing strangers.   The men, too, unlike the Chipeways, (who are of a jealous temper,) eagerly encourage them in this design.   One of the chiefs assured me, that the children, borne by their women to Europeans, were bolder warriors, and better hunters, than themselves.

The Cristinaux have usually two wives each, and often three ; and make no difficulty in lending one of them, for a length of time, to a friend. Some of my men entered into agreements with the respective husbands, in virtue of which they embarked the women in the canoes, promising to return them the next year.   The women, so selected, consider themselves as honoured ; and the husband, who should refuse to lend his wife, would fall under the condemnation of the sex in general.

32

The language of the Cristinaux is a dialect of the Algonquin, and therefore bears some affinity to that of the Chipeway, which is another dialect of the same.   In the north-west, it is commonly called *Cree*, or *Cris.*

CHAPTER IX.

Voyage in the North-West continued. Snow-storm.
River de Bourbon, Pasquayah, or Sascatchiwaine.
Grand Rapide. Lake Winipegon—dimensions,
&c. Lake de Bourbon, or Cedar Lake. Fort
de Bourbon. River Pasquayah. Pasquayah
Village—Traders forced to comply with the de-
mands of the Indians. Cumberland House. Stur-
geon Lake. River Maligne. Beaver Lake.
Build a Fort—and winter in it.

THE Cristinaux made me the usual presents of
wild rice and dried meat, and accompanied them
with the usual formalities. I remained at their village two days, repairing my canoes ; and though
they were drunk the whole time, they behaved very
peaceably, and gave me no annoyance. I observed that two men constantly attended us, and
that these individuals could not be prevailed upon
to taste liquor. They had been assigned us for a
guard ; and they would not allow any drunken Indian to approach our camp.

On the eighteenth of August, I left these amica-
ble people, among whom an intercourse with Euro-

peans appeared to have occasioned less deviation
from their primitive manners, than in any instance
which I had previously discovered. I kept the north
side of the lake, and had not proceeded far before I
was joined by Mr. Pond, a trader of some celebrity
in the north-west. Next day, we encountered a severe gale, from the dangers of which we escaped,
by making the island called the Buffalo's Head;
but, not without the loss of a canoe and four men.
The shores, from the entrance of this lake to the
island, with exception of the points, are rocky and
lofty : the points are rocky, but low.   The wood
is pine and fir.   We took pouts, cat-fish, or cat-
heads, of six pounds weight.

On the twenty-first, we crossed to the south
shore, and reached Oak-point, so called from a few
scrub oaks, which here begin to diversify the forest
of pine and fir.   The pelicans, which we every
where saw, appeared to be impatient of the long
stay we made in fishing.   Leaving the island,
we found the lands along the shore low, and wooded with birch and marsh-maple, intermixed with
spruce-fir.   The beach is gravelly, and the points
rocky.

To the westward of Pike-river, which we passed
on the first of September, is a rock, of great length,
called the Roche Rouge, and entirely composed
of a *pièrre à calumet,* or stone used by the Indians

for making tobacco-pipe bowls. It is of a light red colour, interspersed with veins of brown, and yields very readily to the knife.

On the seventh of September, we were overtaken by Messrs. Joseph and Thomas Frobisher, and Mr. Patterson. On the twentieth, we crossed the bay together, composing a fleet of thirty canoes, and a hundred and thirty men. We were short of provisions.

On the twenty-first, it blew hard, and snow began to fall. The storm continued till the twenty-fifth, by which time the small lakes were frozen over, and two feet of snow lay on level ground, in the woods. This early severity of the season filled us with serious alarms ; for the country was uninhabited for two hundred miles on every side of us, and if detained by winter, our destruction was certain. In this state of peril, we continued our voyage day and night. The fears of our men were a sufficient motive for their exertions.

On the first of October, we gained the mouth of the River de Bourbon, Pasquayah, or Sascatchiwaine,* and proceeded to ascend its stream. The

* The lower part of the Sascatchiwaine was once called the River de Bourbon. *Pasquayah* is the name of an upper portion of the Sascatchiwaine.

Bourbon is a large river, and has its sources to the westward. The lands, which we passed after the twenty-first of September, are more hilly and rocky than those described before. The trees are poplar and spruce. The rocks are chiefly of lime-stone. Our course, from the entrance of Lake Winipegon, was north-west northerly. The lake contains sturgeon ; but, we were not able to take any. At four leagues above the mouth of the river, is the Grand Rapide, two leagues in length, up which the canoes are dragged with ropes. At the end of this is a carrying-place of two miles, through a forest almost uniformly of pine-trees. Here, we met with Indians, fishing for sturgeon. Their practice is, to watch behind the points where the current forms an eddy, in which the sturgeon, coming to rest themselves, are easily speared. The soil is light and sandy. A vessel of any burden might safely navigate Lake Winipegon, from its south-west corner to the Grand Rapide.

Lake Winipegon, or Winipic, or the Lake of the Killistinons, or Cristinaux, empties itself into Hudson's Bay, at Fort York, by a river, sometimes called Port-Nelson River. Its length is said to be one hundred and twenty leagues. Its breadth is unknown. I saw no land, in any direction, after leaving Oak Point.

On the second, we continued our voyage against the current of the Bourbon, which was strong, and interrupted by several *rapids*. On the third, we entered Lake de Bourbon, called by the English, after the Indians, Cedar Lake. This name is derived from the cedar-tree, (*thuya*,) which covers its banks, and which is not found to the northward of this region.

On the fourth, we reached the opposite extremity of Lake de Bourbon. This lake is eighteen leagues in length, and has many deep bays, receding to the northward. The land, by which they are bordered, is in almost all instances out of sight. Several islands, some of which are large, are also in this lake. The shores are generally rocky. At the north end, there was, in the French time, a fort, or trading-house, called Fort de Bourbon, and built by M. de Saint-Pièrre, a French officer, who was the first adventurer into these parts of the country.*

At and adjacent to this fort, are several of the mouths of the river Sascatchiwaine. Here we took several sturgeon, using a seine, the meshes of which were large enough to admit the fish's head, and which we made fast to two canoes.

* In 1766, Carver calls Lake de Bourbon " the most north-
" ward of those yet discovered."

On the sixth, we ascended the Sascatchiwaine, the current of which was here only moderately strong; but, the banks were marshy and overflowed, so that it was with difficulty we found a dry space, large enough to encamp upon. Beaver-lodges were numerous; and the river was every where covered with geese, ducks and other wild fowl. No rising ground was to be seen; and the wood, which was chiefly willow, no where exceeded a man's wrist in thickness.

On the eighth, we resumed our voyage before day-light, making all speed to reach a fishing-place, since winter was very fast approaching. Meeting two canoes of Indians, we engaged them to accompany us, as hunters. The number of ducks and geese which they killed was absolutely prodigious.

At eighty leagues above Fort de Bourbon, at the head of a stream which falls into the Sascatchiwaine, and into which we had turned, we found the Pasquayah village. It consisted of thirty families, lodged in tents of a circular form, and composed of dressed ox-skins, stretched upon poles twelve feet in length, and leaning against a stake driven into the ground in the centre.

On our arrival, the chief, named Chatique, or The Pelican, came down upon the beach, attended

by thirty followers, all armed with the bows and arrows, and with spears. Chatique was a man of
more than six feet in height, somewhat corpulent,
and of a very doubtful physiognomy. He invited
us to his tent ; and we observed that he was particularly anxious to bestow his hospitalities on those
who were the owners of the goods. We suspected
an evil design ; but, judged it better to lend ourselves to the treachery, than to discover fear. We
entered the lodge accordingly, and soon perceived
that we were surrounded by armed men.

Chatique presently rose up, and told us, that he
was glad to see us arrive; that the young men of the
village, as well as himself, had long been in want of
many things of which we were possessed in abundance ; that we must be well aware of his power to
prevent our going further ; that if we passed now,
he could put us all to death on our return ; and
that under these circumstances, he expected us to
be exceedingly liberal in our presents : adding,
that to avoid misunderstanding, he would inform
us of what it was that he must have. It consisted
in three casks of gunpowder ; four bags of shot and
ball ; two bales of tobacco ; three kegs of rum, and
three guns ; together with knives, flints and some
smaller articles. He went on to say, that he had
before now been acquainted with white men, and

knew that they promised more than they performed ; that with the number of men which he had,
he could take the whole of our property, without
our consent ; and that therefore his demands ought
to be regarded as very reasonable : that he was a
peaceable man, and one that contented himself
with moderate views, in order to avoid quarrels ;—
finally, that he desired us to signify our assent to
his proposition, before we quitted our places.

The men in the canoes exceeded the Indians in
number ; but, they were unarmed, and without a
leader : our consultation was therefore short, and
we promised to comply. This done, the pipe was
handed round as usual ; and the omission of this
ceremony, on our entrance, had sufficiently marked
the intentions of Chatique. The pipe dismissed,
we obtained permission to depart, for the purpose
of assorting the presents ; and, these bestowed, or
rather yielded up, we hastened away from the
plunderers.

We had supposed the affair finished ; but, before we had proceeded two miles, we saw a canoe
behind us. On this, we dropped astern, to give
the canoes that were following us an opportunity
of joining, lest, being alone, they should be insulted. Presently, however, Chatique, in a solitary
canoe, rushed into the midst of our squadron, and

boarded one of our canoes, spear in hand, demand-
ing a keg of rum, and threatening to put to death
the first that opposed him.   We saw that our only
alternative was, to kill this daring robber, or to submit to his exaction.   The former part would have
been attended with very mischievous consequences ; and we therefore curbed our indignation, and
chose the latter.   On receiving the rum, he saluted
us with the Indian cry, and departed.

Every day, we were on the water before dawn,
and paddled along till dark.   The nights were
frosty ; and no provisions, excepting a few wild
fowl, were to be procured.   We were in daily fear
that our progress would be arrested by the ice.

On the twenty-sixth, we reached Cumberland
House, one of the factories of the Hudson's Bay
Company,   seated on Sturgeon Lake, in about 54?
north latitude, and 102° longitude west from Green-
wich.   This house had been built the year before,
by Mr. Hearne, who was now absent, on his well-
known journey of discovery.   We found it garrisoned by Highlanders, from the Orkney Islands, and
under the command of a Mr. Cockings, by whom,
though unwelcome guests, we were treated with
much civility.   The design, in building this house,
was to prevent the Indians from dealing with the
Canadian merchants, and to induce them to go to

Hudson's Bay. It is distant one hundred leagues from Chatique's village ; and of this space the first fifty leagues comprise lands nearly level with the water ; but, in the latter, the surface is more lofty, rising a hundred feet above the river, and increasing in height as we advance. The soil is a white clay, mixed with sand. The wood is small and scanty.

At Cumberland House, the canoes separated ; M. Cadotte going with four to Fort des Prairies ; Mr. Pond, with two, to Fort Dauphin ; and others proceeding on still different routes. Messrs. Frobisher retained six, and myself four ; and we resolved on joining our stock, and wintering together. We steered for the river Churchill, or Missinipi, to the east of Beaver Lake, or Lake aux Castors.

Sturgeon Lake, which we now crossed, is twenty leagues in length. On the east are high lands, and on the west, low islands. The river Maligne falls into it. This we ascended, but not without much labour, from the numerous *rapids*, on account of which, the Canadians, in their vexation, have given it the name it bears.

We crossed Beaver Lake on the first day of November ; and the very next morning it was frozen

over. Happily, we were now at a place abounding
with fish ; and here, therefore, we resolved on wintering.

Our first object was to procure food. We had
only three days' stock remaining, and we were
forty-three persons in number. Our forty men
were divided into three parties, of which two were
detached to the River aux Castors, on which the ice
was strong enough to allow of setting the nets, in
the manner heretofore described. The third party
was employed in building our house, or fort ;
and, in this, within ten days, we saw ourselves
commodiously lodged. Indeed, we had almost
built a village ; or, in soberer terms, we had
raised buildings round a quadrangle, such as really
assumed, in the wilds which encompassed it, a
formidable appearance. In front, was the house
designed for Messrs. Frobisher and myself ; and
the men had four houses, of which one was placed
on each side, and two in the rear.

Our canoes were disposed of on scaffolds ; for,
the ground being frozen, we could not bury them,
as is the usual practice, and which is done to pro-
tect them from that severity of cold which occasions the bark to contract and split.

The houses being finished, we divided the men anew, making four parties, of nine each. Four were retained as wood-cutters ; and each party was to provide for its own subsistence.

Our fishing was very successful. We took trout of the weight of from ten to fifty pounds ; white-fish of five pounds ; and pike of the usual size. There were also pickerel, called *poissons dorés,* (gilt-fish,) and sturgeon; but, of the last, we caught only one. The Indians, soon after our arrival, killed two elks, otherwise called *moose-deer.**

Lake aux Castors, or Beaver Lake, is seven leagues in length, and from three to five in breadth. It has several islands, of which the largest does not exceed a mile in circumference. The lands on either shore are mountainous and rocky.

Messrs. Frobisher and myself were continually employed in fishing. We made holes in the ice, and took trout with the line, in twenty and thirty fathom water, using white-fish, of a pound weight, for our bait, which we sunk to the bottom, or very near it.

* Cervus alces.

In this manner, I have at times caught more than twenty large trout a-day ; but, my more usual mode was that of spearing. By one means or other, fish was plenty with us ; but, we suffered severely from the cold, in fishing. On the twenty-fifth, the frost was so excessive, that we had nearly perished. Fahrenheit's thermometer was at 32º below zero in the shade ; the mercury contracted one eighth, and for four days did not rise into the tube.

Several Indians brought beaver and bear's meat, and some skins, for sale. Their practice was, to remain with us one night, and leave us in the morning.

CHAPTER X.

*Winter journey from Beaver Lake to the Plains,
or Prairies. Author accompanied to Cumberland House by Mr. Joseph Frobisher—reaches
the Pasquayah, or Sascatchiwaine. Snow storm.
Provisions exhausted—and consequent sufferings.
Fort des Prairies. Plains—reports of their
boundaries—inhabitants. Osinipoilles, or Assiniboins. Author joins a party of Osinipoilles, and
accompanies them to their Village.*

THE Plains, or, as the French denominate them,
the Prairies, or Meadows, compose an extensive
tract of country, which is watered by the Elk, or
Athabasca, the Sascatchiwaine, the Red River and
others, and runs southward to the Gulf of Mexico.
On my first setting out for the north-west, I promised myself to visit this region, and I now prepared
to accomplish the undertaking. Long journies,
on the snow, are thought of but as trifles, in this
part of the world.

On the first day of January, 1776, I left our fort
on Beaver Lake, attended by two men, and provi-

ded with dried meat, frozen fish, and a small
quantity of *praline*, made of roasted maize, rendered palatable with sugar, and which I had
brought from the Sault de Sainte-Marie, for this
express occasion. The kind and friendly disposition of Mr. Joseph Frobisher, induced him to bear
me company, as far as Cumberland House, a journey of a hundred and twenty miles. Mr. Frobisher
was attended by one man.

Our provisions were drawn by the men, upon
sledges, made of thin boards, a foot in breadth, and
curved upward in front, after the Indian fashion.
Our clothing for night and day was nearly the
same ; and the cold was so intense, that exclusively
of warm woollen clothes, we were obliged to wrap
ourselves continually in beaver blankets, or at least
in ox-skins, which the traders call *buffalo-robes*. At
night, we made our first encampment at the head of
the Maligne, where one of our parties was fishing,
with but very indifferent success.

On the following evening, we encamped at the
mouth of the same river. The snow was four feet
deep ; and we found it impossible to keep ourselves warm, even with the aid of a large fire.

On the fourth day, as well of the month as of
our journey, we arrived at Cumberland House.
Mr. Cockings received us with much hospitality,

making us partake of all he had, which, however, was but little. Himself and his men subsisted wholly upon fish, in which sturgeon bore the largest proportion ; and this was caught near the house. The next morning, I took leave of Mr. Frobisher, who is certainly the first man that ever went the same distance, in such a climate, and upon snow-shoes, to convoy a friend !

From Cumberland House, I pursued a westerly course, on the ice, following the southern bank of Sturgeon Lake, till I crossed the neck of land by which alone it is separated from the great river Pasquayah, or Sascatchiwaine. In the evening, I encamped on the north bank of this river, at the distance of ten leagues from Cumberland House.

The depth of the snow, and the intenseness of the cold, rendered my progress so much slower than I had reckoned upon, that I soon began to fear the want of provisions. The sun did not rise till half past nine o'clock in the morning, and it set at half past two in the afternoon : it is, however, at no time wholly dark in these climates ; the north-ern lights, and the reflection of the snow, affording always sufficient light for the traveller. Add to this, that the river, the course of which I was ascending, was a guide, with the aid of which I could not lose my way. Every day's journey was commenced at three o'clock in the morning.

I was not far advanced, before the country betrayed some approaches to the characteristic nakedness of the Plains. The wood dwindled away, both in size and quantity, so that it was with difficulty we could collect sufficient for making a fire, and without fire we could not drink; for melted snow was our only resource, the ice on the river being too thick to be penetrated by the axe.

On the evening of the sixth, the weather continuing severely cold, I made my two men sleep on the same skin with myself, one on each side ; and though this arrangement was particularly beneficial to myself, it increased the comfort of all. At the usual hour in the morning, we attempted to rise ; but found that a foot of snow had fallen upon our bed, as well as extinguished and covered our fire. In this situation we remained till day-break, when, with much exertion, we collected fresh fuel. Proceeding on our journey, we found that the use of our sledges had become impracticable, through the quantity of newly fallen snow, and were now constrained to carry our provisions on our backs. Unfortunately, they were a diminished burden !

For the two days succeeding, the depth of the snow, and the violence of the winds, greatly retarded our journey ; but, from the ninth to the twelfth, the elements were less hostile, and we travelled rapidly.   No trace of any thing human presented itself on our road, except that we saw the old wintering-ground of Mr. Finlay, who had left it some years before, and was now stationed at Fort des Prairies.   This fort was the stage we had to make, before we could enter the Prairies, or Plains; and on examining our provisions, we found only sufficient for five days, while, even at the swiftest rate we had travelled, a journey of twelve days was before us.   My men began to fear being starved, as seeing no prospect of relief; but, I endeavoured to maintain their courage, by representing that I should certainly kill red-deer and elk, of which the tracks were visible along the banks of the river, and on the sides of the hills. What I hoped for, in this respect, it was not easy to accomplish ; for the animals kept within the shelter of the woods, and the snow was too deep to let me seek them there.

On the fifteenth, our situation was rendered still more alarming, by the commencement of a fresh fall of snow, which added nearly two feet to the depth of that which was on the ground before.   At the same time, we were scarcely able to collect enough wood for making a fire to melt the snow. The only trees around us were starveling willows ; and the hills, which discovered themselves at a small distance, were bare of every vegetable production, such as could rear itself above

the snow. Their appearance was rather that of
lofty snow-banks, than of hills. We were now on
the borders of the Plains.

On the twentieth, the last remains of our provisions were expended ; but, I had taken the precaution to conceal a cake of chocolate, in reserve
for an occasion like that which was now arrived. Toward evening, my men, after walking the
whole day, began to lose their strength ; but, we
nevertheless kept on our feet till it was late ; and,
when we encamped, I informed them of the treasure which was still in store. I desired them to fill
the kettle with snow, and argued with them the
while, that the chocolate would keep us alive, for
five days at least ; an interval in which we should
surely meet with some Indian at the chase. Their
spirits revived at the suggestion ; and, the kettle
being filled with two gallons of water, I put into it
one square of the chocolate. The quantity was
scarcely sufficient to alter the colour of the water ;
but, each of us drank half a gallon of the warm liquor, by which we were much refreshed, and in its
enjoyment felt no more of the fatigues of the day. In
the morning, we allowed ourselves a similar repast,
after finishing which, we marched vigorously for
six hours. But, now, the spirits of my companions
again deserted them, and they declared, that they
neither would, nor could, proceed any further. For
myself, they advised me to leave them, and ac-

complish the journey as I could ; but, for themselves, they said, that they must die soon, and might
as well die where they were, as any where else.

While things were in this melancholy posture,
I filled the kettle, and boiled another square of
chocolate. When prepared, I prevailed upon my
desponding companions to return to their warm
beverage. On taking it, they recovered incon-
ceivably ; and, after smoking a pipe, consented to
go forward. While their stomachs were comfort-
ed by the warm water, they walked well ; but, as
evening approached, fatigue overcame them, and
they relapsed into their former condition ; and, the
chocolate being now almost entirely consumed, I
began to fear that I must really abandon them :
for I was able to endure more hardship than they ;
and, had it not been for keeping company with
them, I could have advanced, double the distance,
within the time which had been spent. To my
great joy, however, the usual quantity of warm water revived them.

For breakfast, the next morning, I put the last
square of chocolate into the kettle ; and our meal
finished, we began our march, in but very indifferent spirits. We were surrounded by large herds
of wolves, which sometimes came close upon us,
and who knew, as we were prone to think, the extremity in which we were, and marked us for their

prey ; but, I carried a gun, and this was our protection. I fired several times, but unfortunately missed
at each ; for a morsel of wolf's flesh would have
afforded us a banquet.

Our misery, nevertheless, was still nearer
its end than we imagined ; and the event was
such as to give one of the innumerable proofs, that
despair is not made for man. Before sunset, we
discovered, on the ice, some remains of the bones
of an elk, left there by the wolves. Having instantly gathered them, we encamped ; and, filling
our kettle, prepared ourselves a meal of strong and
excellent soup. The greater part of the night was
passed in boiling and regaling on our booty ; and
early in the morning we felt ourselves strong
enough to proceed.

This day, the twenty-fifth, we found the borders
of the Plains reaching to the very banks of the
river, which were two hundred feet above the level
of the ice. Water-marks presented themselves at
twenty feet above the actual level.

Want had lost his dominion over us. At noon,
we saw the horns of a red-deer, standing in the
snow, on the river. On examination, we found that
the whole carcass was with them, the animal having broke through the ice in the beginning of the
winter, in attempting to cross the river, too early in

the season ; while his horns, fastening themselves
in the ice, had prevented him from sinking.   By
cutting away the ice, we were enabled to lay bare a
part of the back and shoulders, and thus procure a
stock of food, amply sufficient for the rest of
our journey.   We accordingly encamped, and employed our kettle to good purpose ; forgot all our
misfortunes ; and prepared to walk with cheerful-
ness the twenty leagues, which, as we reckoned,
still lay between ourselves and Fort des Prairies.

Though the deer must have been in this situation ever since the month of November, yet its
flesh was perfectly good.   Its horns alone were five
foot high, or more ; and it will therefore not appear
extraordinary, that they should be seen above the
snow.

On the twenty-seventh, in the morning, we discovered the print of snow-shoes, demonstrating
that several persons had passed that way the day
before. These were the first marks of other human
feet than our own, which we had seen since our
leaving Cumberland House ; and it was much to
feel, that we had fellow-creatures in the wide waste
surrounding us !   In the evening, we reached the
fort.

At Fort des Prairies, I remained several days,
hospitably entertained by my friends, who covered

their table with the tongues and marrow of wild bulls. The quantity of provisions, which I found collected here, exceeded every thing of which I had previously formed a notion. In one heap, I saw fifty ton of beef, so fat that the men could scarcely find a sufficiency of lean.

I had come to see the Plains ; and I had yet a serious journey to perform, in order to gratify my curiosity. Their southern boundary I have already named ; and I understood that they stretched northward, to the sixtieth degree of north latitude, and westward, to the feet of the Rocky Mountains, or Northern Andes, of which the great chain pursues a north-westerly direction. The mountains, seen in high latitudes, were regarded as parts of this chain, and said to be inhabited by numerous bands of Indians. The Plains cross the river Pasquayah, Kejeeche-won, Sascatchiwaine or Shascatchiwan, a little above Fort des Prairies.

The Indians, who inhabit them immediately to the southward, are called Osinipoilles, or Assiniboins. At the fort, I met with a woman who was a slave among the Osinipoilles, taken far to the westward of the mountains, in a country which the latter incessantly ravage. She informed me, that the men of the country never suffer themselves to be taken, but always die in the field, rather than fall into captivity. The women and

35

children are made slaves, but are not put to death, nor tormented.* Her nation lived on a great river, running to the south-west, and cultivated beans, squashes, maize and tobacco. The lands were generally mountainous, and covered with pine and fir. She had heard of men who wear their beards. She had been taken in one of the incursions of the Osinipoilles. Of the men who were in the village, the greater part were killed ; but, a few escaped, by swimming across the river.

The woman belonged to a numerous band of Osinipoilles, which was at the fort, selling its meat and skins. I resolved on travelling with these people, to their village ; and accordingly set out on the fifth of February, accompanied by Messrs. Patterson and Holmes, and attended by my two Canadians.

* The Five Nations, and others, are known to have treated their prisoners with great cruelty ; but, there is too much reason to believe, that the exercise of this cruelty has been often encouraged, and its malignity often increased, by European instigators and assistants.

CHAPTER XI.

Journey on the Plains, from Fort des Prairies to a Village of the Osinipoilles. Table-land. Moose-river. Red-deer. Winter appearance of the Plains. Danger from drifted Snow. Coppices, or Islands. Wild Oxen. Messengers from Great Chief. Snow-storm—and Herd of Oxen. Tobacco highly esteemed among the Indians. Encamp near the Village. Entry. Guard of Honour. Tent assigned to the Strangers.

WE departed at an early hour, and after a march of about two miles, ascended the table-land, which lies above the river, and of which the level is two hundred feet higher than that of the land on which the fort is built. From the low ground upward, the soil is covered with poplar, of a large growth; but, the summit of the ridge is no sooner gained, than the wood is found to be smaller, and so thinly scattered, that a wheel-carriage might pass, in any direction. At noon, we crossed a small river, called Moose-river, flowing at the feet of very lofty banks. Moose-river is said to fall into Lake Dauphin.

Beyond this stream, the wood grows still more scanty, and the land more and more level. Our course was southerly. The snow lay four feet deep. The Indians travelled swiftly; and, in keeping pace with them, my companions and myself had too much exercise, to suffer from the coldness of the atmosphere; but, our snow-shoes being of a broader make than those of the Indians, we had much fatigue in following their track. The women led, and we marched till sunset, when we reached a small coppice of wood, under the protection of which we encamped. The baggage of the Indians was drawn by dogs, who kept pace with the women, and appeared to be under their command. As soon as we halted, the women set up the tents, which were constructed, and covered, like those of the Cristinaux.

The tent, in which I slept, contained fourteen persons, each of whom lay with his feet to the fire, which was in the middle; but, the night was so cold, that even this precaution, with the assistance of our *buffalo-robes*, was insufficient to keep us warm. Our supper was made cn the tongues of the wild ox, or buffalo, boiled in my kettle, which was the only one in the camp.

At break of day, or rather before that time, we left our encampment; the women still preceding us. On our march, we saw but little wood, and that

only here and there, and at great distances. We
crossed two rivulets, stealing along the bottom
of very deep channels, which, no doubt, are better
filled in the season of the melting of the snow. The
banks here, as on the Pasquayah, or Sascatchiwaine, are composed of a whitish clay, mingled
with sand.

On the sixth of February, we had a fine clear
sky ; but, the air was exceedingly cold and bleak,
no shelter from woods being afforded us, on either
side. There was but little wind, and yet, at times,
enough to cause a slight drift of snow. In the
evening, we encamped in a small wood, of which
the largest trees did not exceed a man's wrist in
thickness. On the seventh, we left our encampment at an early hour. Tracks of large herds of
animals presented themselves, which the Indians
said were those of red-deer. Our course was
south-west, and the weather very cold. The country was one uninterrupted plain, in many parts of
which no wood, nor even the smallest shrub, was
to be seen : a continued level, without a single
eminence ; a frozen sea, of which the little coppices were the islands. That, behind which we had
encamped the night before, soon sunk in the horizon ; and the eye had nothing left, save only the
sky and snow. The latter was still four feet in
depth.

At noon, we discovered, and presently passed by, a diminutive wood, or island. At four in the afternoon, another was in sight. When I could see none, I was alive to the danger to be feared from a storm of wind, which would have driven the snow upon us. The Indians related, that whole families often perish in this manner.

It was dark before we reached the wood. A fire, of which we had much need, was soon kindled by the women. Axes were useless here; for the largest tree yielded easily to the hand. It was not only small, but in a state of decay, and easily extracted from the loose soil in which it grew. We supped on wild beef and snow-water. In the night, the wind changed to the southward, and the weather became milder. I was still asleep, when the women began their noisy preparations for our march. The striking of the tents, the tongues of the women, and the cries of the dogs, were all heard at once. At the first dawn of day, we recommenced our journey. Nothing was visible but the snow and sky; and the snow was drifted into ridges, resembling waves.

Soon after sunrise, we descried a herd of oxen, extending a mile and a half in length, and too numerous to be counted. They travelled, not one after another, as, in the snow, other animals usually do, but, in a broad phalanx, slowly, and sometimes stopping to feed. We did not disturb them ; because to have attacked them would have occasioned much delay to our progress ; and because the dogs were already sufficiently burdened, not to need the addition of the spoil.

At two o'clock, we reached a small lake, surrounded with wood, and where the trees were of a size somewhat larger than those behind. There were birch-trees among the rest. I observed, that wherever there was water, there was wood. All the snow upon the lake was trodden down by the feet of wild oxen. When this was the case on the land, an abundance of coarse grass discovered itself beneath. We were unable to penetrate to the water in the lake, though we cut a hole in the ice, to the depth of three feet. Where we cleared the ground for our encampments, no stones were to be seen.

This evening, we had scarcely encamped, when there arrived two Osinipoilles, sent by the great chief of the nation, whose name was the Great Road, to meet the troop. The chief had been induced to send them through his anxiety, occasioned by their longer absence than had been expected. The messengers expressed themselves much pleased at finding strangers with their friends, and told us, that we were within one day's march of their village, and that the great chief would be highly gratified, in learning the long journey which we had

performed to visit him. They added, that in consequence of finding us, they must themselves return
immediately, to apprise him of our coming, and
enable him to prepare for our reception.

Fortunately, they had not been able to take any
refreshment, before a storm of wind and snow commenced, which prevented their departure, and in
which they must have been lost, had it happened
later. The storm continued all the night, and part
of the next day. Clouds of snow, raised by the
wind, fell on the encampment, and almost buried it.
I had no resource but in my buffalo-robe.

In the morning, we were alarmed by the approach of a herd of oxen, who came from the
open ground, to shelter themselves in the wood.
Their numbers were so great, that we dreaded lest
they should fairly trample down the camp ; nor
could it have happened otherwise, but for the dogs,
almost as numerous as they, who were able to
keep them in check. The Indians killed several,
when close upon their tents ; but, neither the fire
of the Indians, nor the noise of the dogs, could
soon drive them away. Whatever were the terrors which filled the wood, they had no other
escape from the terrors of the storm.

In the night of the tenth, the wind fell. The
interval had been passed in feasting on the tongues

of the oxen.   On the morning of the eleventh, the
messengers left us before day-light.   We had
already charged them with a present for the chief,
consisting in tobacco and vermilion.   Of these articles, the former exceeds all others in estimation :
for the Indians are universally great smokers, men,
women and children ; and no affair can be trans-
acted, civil or religious, without the pipe.

Our march was performed at a quick pace, in
the track of the messengers.   All the fore part of
the day escaped, without discovering to us a single
wood, or even a single twig, with the exception of
a very small island, lying on our right ; but, at
four o'clock in the afternoon, we reached a little
scrub, or bushy tract, on which we encamped. We
were at no great distance from the village ; but,
the Indians, as is their custom, delayed their entry
till the morning.

On the twelfth, at ten o'clock in the forenoon,
we were in sight of a wood, or island, as the term
not unnaturally is, as well with the Indians as
others : it appeared to be about a mile and a half
long.   Shortly after, we observed smoke rising
from it, and were informed that it was the smoke
of the village.   The morning was clear, and the
sun shining.

At eleven o'clock, two fresh messengers came from the village, by whom the strangers were formally welcomed, on the part of the chief. They told us, that they were directed to conduct us and our servants to a lodge, which had been prepared for our reception.

At the entrance of the wood, we were met by a large band of Indians, having the appearance of a guard; each man being armed with his bow and spear, and having his quiver filled with arrows. In this, as in much that followed, there was more of order and discipline, than in any thing which I had before witnessed among Indians. The power of these guards appeared to be great; for they treated very roughly some of the people, who, in their opinion, approached us too closely. Forming themselves in regular file, on either side of us, they escorted us to the lodge, or tent, which was assigned us. It was of a circular form, covered with leather, and not less than twenty feet in diameter. On the ground within, ox-skins were spread, for beds and seats.

CHAPTER XII.

Hospitality and Ceremony of the Osinipoilles. Feast given by the Great Chief. The Pipe, or Calumet. Weeping. Remarkable Superstition. Second Feast. Orderly demeanour of the Guard. Camp, or Village, always on the alert. Number of Tents and Families. Curiosity of the Inhabitants. Dogs. Horses. Visit of the Great Chief— Retinue—Speech—and Present. Great Chief designs to visit the Fort. Third Feast. Daily Feasts. Domestic Order. Military Police. Hunting the Wild Ox proposed.

ONE half of the tent was appropriated to our use. Several women waited upon us, to make a fire, and bring water, which latter they fetched from a neighbouring tent. Shortly after our arrival, these women brought us water, unasked for, saying that it was for washing. The refreshment was exceedingly acceptable; for, on our march, we had become so dirty, that our complexions were not very distinguishable from those of the Indians themselves.

The same women presently borrowed our kettle, telling us, that they wanted to boil something for us to eat. Soon after, we heard the voice of a man, passing through the village, and making a speech as he went. Our interpreter informed us, that his speech contained an invitation to a feast, accompanied by a proclamation, in which the people were required to behave with decorum toward the strangers, and apprised, that the soldiers had orders to punish those who should do otherwise.

While we were procuring this explanation, an Indian, who appeared to be a chief, came into our tent, and invited us to the feast ; adding, that he would himself show us the way. We followed him accordingly, and he carried us to the tent of the great chief, which we found neither more ornamented, nor better furnished, than the rest.

At our entrance, the chief arose from his seat, saluted us in the Indian manner, by shaking hands, and addressed us in a few words, in which he offered his thanks for the confidence which we had reposed in him, in trusting ourselves so far from our own country. After we were seated, which was on bear-skins, spread on the ground, the pipe, as usual, was introduced, and presented in succession to each person present. Each took his whiff, and then let it pass to his neighbour.   The stem, which was four feet in length, was held by an officer, attendant on the chief.   The bowl was of red marble, or pipe-stone.

When the pipe had gone its round, the chief, without rising from his seat, delivered a speech of some length, but of which the general purport was of the nature already described, in speaking of the Indians of the Lake of the Woods.*   The speech ended, several of the Indians began to weep, and they were soon joined by the whole party. Had I not previously been witness to a *weeping-scene* of this description, I should certainly have been apprehensive of some disastrous catastrophe ; but, as it was, I listened to it with tranquillity.   It lasted for about ten minutes, after which all tears were dried away, and the honours of the feast were performed by the attending chiefs.   This consisted in giving to every guest a dish, containing a boiled wild ox's tongue—for preparing which, my kettle had been borrowed.   The repast finished, the great chief dismissed us, by shaking hands ; and we returned to our tent.

Having inquired among these people, why they always weep at their feasts, and sometimes at their

---

* See Part II. Chapter 8.

councils, I was answered, that their tears flowed to the memory of those deceased relations, who formerly assisted both at the one and the other ;—that their absence, on these occasions, necessarily brought them fresh into their minds, and at the same time led them to reflect on their own brief and uncertain continuance.*

The chief to whose kindly reception we were so much indebted, was about five feet ten inches high, and of a complexion rather darker than that of the Indians in general. His appearance was greatly injured by the condition of his head of hair, and this was the result of an extraordinary superstition.

The Indians universally fix upon a particular object, as sacred to themselves ; as the giver of their prosperity, and as their preserver from evil. The choice is determined either by a dream, or by some strong predilection of fancy ; and usually falls upon an animal, or part of an animal, or something else which is to be met with, by land, or by water : but, the Great Road had made choice of his hair—placing, like Sampson, all his safety in this portion of his proper substance !   His

---

* The Osinipoilles are the *Issati* of the older travellers, and have sometimes been called the *Weepers*.

hair was the fountain of all his happiness ; it was
his strength and his weapon, his spear and his
shield.   It preserved him in battle, directed him in
the chase, watched over him in the march, and
gave length of days to his wives and children.
Hair, of a quality like this, was not to be pro-
faned by the touch of human hands.   I was assured, that it had never been cut, nor combed,
from his childhood upward ; and, that when any
part of it fell from his head, he treasured up that
part with care : meanwhile, it did not escape all
care, even while growing on the head ; but, was in
the special charge of a spirit, who dressed it while
the owner slept. All this might be; but, the spirit's
style of hair-dressing was at least peculiar ; the
hair being suffered to remain very much as if it
received no dressing at all, and matted into ropes,
which spread themselves in all directions.

The same evening, we were invited to a second
feast.   Every thing was nearly as before, except
that in the morning all the guests were men, and
now half were women.   All the women were seated on one side of the floor of the tent, and all the
men on the other, with a fire placed between them.
The fire rendering the tent warm, the men, one
after another, dropped the skins which were their
garments, and left themselves entirely naked.   The
appearance of one of them in particular, having led

us, who were strangers, into an involuntary and ill-
stifled laugh, the men calmly asked us the occasion
of our mirth ; but, one of the women pointing to
the cause, the individual restored the covering of
his robe.

The women are themselves perfectly modest,
both in dress and demeanour ; and those, who were
now present, maintained the first rank in the village ;
but, custom had rendered the scene inoffensive to
their eyes.

Our repast concluded, we departed, taking with
us our dishes, in which the greater part of the ox-
tongues, which had been laid upon them, remained
unconsumed.

All night, in our tent, we had a guard of six soldiers ; and, when I awoke, as several times I did,
I always found them smoking their pipes in silence.

We rose at day-break, according to the custom
of the Indians, who say, that they follow it in order
to avoid surprises; this being the hour at which the
enemy uniformly makes his attack.

Our waiting-women arrived early, bringing
wood and water. Washing appeared to me to be

a ceremony of religion among the Osinipoilles ; and I never saw any thing similar among other Indians.

Leaving our tent, we made a progress through the village, which consisted of about two hundred tents, each tent containing from two to four families. We were attended by four soldiers of our guard, but this was insufficient for keeping off the women and children, who crowded round us with insatiable curiosity. Our march was likewise accompanied by a thousand dogs, all howling frightfully.

From the village, I saw, for the first time, one of those herds of horses which the Osinipoilles possess in numbers. It was feeding on the skirts of the plain. The masters of these herds provide them with no fodder ; but, leave them to find food for themselves, by removing the snow with their feet, till they reach the grass, which is every where on the ground in plenty.

At ten o'clock, we returned to our tent, and in a short time the great chief paid us a visit, attended by nearly fifty followers of distinction. In coming in, he gave his hand to each of us, and all his attendants followed his example. When we were seated, one of the officers went through the ceremony of the pipe, after which, the great chief deli-

vered a speech, of which the substance was as fol-
lows: That he was glad to see us; that he had been,
some time since, informed of a fort of the white-
men's being established on the Pasquayah, and
that it had always been his intention to pay a visit
there; that we were our own masters, to remain at
our pleasure in his village, free from molestation,
and assured of his especial protection; that the
young men had employed themselves in collecting
meat and furs, for the purpose of purchasing certain articles, wherewith to decorate their wives;
that within a few days he proposed to move, with
his whole village, on this errand; that nothing
should be omitted to make our stay as agreeable
as possible; that he had already ordered a party of
his soldiers to guard us, and that if any thing
should occur to displease us, his ear was always
open to our complaints.

For all these friendly communications, we offered our thanks. His visit to the fort it had been a
principal object to invite.

After the speech, the chief presented us with
twenty beaver-skins, and as many wolf. In return,
we gave two pounds of vermilion, and a few fathom
of twisted tobacco, assuring him, that when he
should arrive at our habitation, we would endeavour to repay the benefits which we were receiving
from him, and at the same time cheerfully exchange

our merchandise, for the dried meat and skins of his village. It was agreed that he should strike his camp at the end of five days, and that we should remain in it so long, and accompany it to the fort. The chief now departed ; and I believe that we were reciprocally pleased with each other.

A short time after he was gone, we received an invitation to a feast, from a subordinate chief. Our dishes were again filled with tongues, but roasted, and not boiled. To furnish us with water, we saw an ox's paunch employed as a kettle. This being hung in the smoke of a fire, was filled with snow ; and, as the snow melted, more was added, till the paunch was full of water. The lower orifice of the organ was used for drawing off the water, and stopped with a plug and string.

During our whole stay, we never had occasion for cookery at home ; but, my kettle was in constant use, and for the most part in preparation of the feasts at which we were daily guests. In our tent, we were regularly supplied with water, either by the women, or by the guards.

The guards were changed daily. They frequently beat the people, for disobedience of orders, and the offenders made no resistance to the chastisement. We were informed, that there was at both extremities of the camp, or village, a picket

of two men, whose duty it was not to allow any
person to go beyond the bounds.   The intention of
this was to prevent stragglers from falling a prey
to the enemy.   General orders were issued by the
chief, morning and evening, and published by a
crier, in every part of the camp.

   In the course of the day, the great chief informed us, that he proposed hunting the wild ox on the
following morning, and invited us to be of the
party.

CHAPTER XIII.

Wild Ox Hunt. Dances and Festivity. Musical Instruments. Some account of the Plains—Inhabitants to the Westward. Weapons of War. Horses originally procured from the Spaniards. Religious notions and practices—Songs—Feasts —Fasts—Dances—Sacrifices. Agreement, in these and other particulars, between the Osinipoilles and Cristinaux. Marriages of the Indians in general.—Courtship—Contracts of Marriage. Stews, Sudatories, or Sweating-Houses. Polygamy. Paucity of Children. Burial of the Dead. Manes. Food placed on Graves. Monuments. Persons of the Osinipoilles. Dress of the Women. Cruel treatment of Slaves.

IN the morning, we went to the hunt accordingly. The chief was followed by about forty men, and a great number of women. We proceeded to a small *island* on the plain, at the distance of five miles from the village. On our way, we saw large herds of oxen, at feed ; but, the hunters forbore to molest them, lest they should take the alarm.

Arrived at the island, the women pitched a few tents, while the chief led his hunters to its southern end, where there was a pound, or enclosure. The fence was about four feet high, and formed of strong stakes of birch-wood, wattled with smaller branches of the same. The day was spent in making repairs; and by the evening all was ready for the hunt.

At day-light, several of the more expert hunters were sent to decoy the animals into the pound. They were dressed in ox-skins, with the hair and horns. Their faces were covered, and their gestures so closely resembled those of the animals themselves, that had I not been in the secret, I should have been as much deceived as the oxen.

At ten o'clock, one of the hunters returned, bringing information of the herd. Immediately, all the dogs were muzzled; and this done, the whole crowd of men and women surrounded the outside of the pound. The herd, of which the extent was so great that I cannot pretend to estimate the numbers, was distant half a mile, advancing slowly, and frequently stopping to feed. The part, played by the decoyers, was that of approaching them within hearing, and then bellowing like themselves. On hearing the noise, the oxen did not fail to give it attention; and, whether from curiosity or sympathy, advanced to meet those from whom it proceeded. These, in the mean time, fell back deliberately toward the pound, always repeating the call, whenever the oxen stopped. This was reiterated till the leaders of the herd had followed the decoyers into the jaws of the pound, which, though wide asunder toward the plain, terminated, like a funnel, in a small aperture, or gate-way; and, within this, was the pound itself. The Indians remark, that in all herds of animals there are chiefs, or leaders, by whom the motions of the rest are determined.

The decoyers now retired within the pound, and were followed by the oxen. But, the former retired still further, withdrawing themselves at certain movable parts of the fence, while the latter were fallen upon by all the hunters, and presently wounded, and killed, by showers of arrows. Amid the uproar which ensued, the oxen made several attempts to force the fence ; but, the Indians stopped them, and drove them back, by shaking skins before their eyes. Skins were also made use of to stop the entrance, being let down by strings, as soon as the oxen were inside. The slaughter was prolonged till the evening, when the hunters returned to their tents. Next morning, all the tongues were presented to the chief, to the number of seventy-two.

The women brought the meat to the village, on sledges drawn by dogs. The lumps on the shoul-

ders, and the hearts, as well as the tongues, were
set apart for feasts ; while the rest was consumed
as ordinary food, or dried, for sale at the fort.

II. The time was now passed in dancing and
festivity, in all quarters of the village. On the evening of the day after the hunt, the chief came to our
tent, bringing with him about twenty men, and as
many women, who seated separately themselves as
before; but, they now brought musical instruments,
and, soon after their arrival, began to play. The
instruments consisted principally in a sort of tam-
bourine, and a gourd filled with stones, which
several persons accompanied by shaking two
bones together ; and others with bunches of deer-
hoofs, fastened to the end of a stick. Another instrument was one that was no more than a piece of
wood, of three feet, with notches cut on its edge.
The performer drew a stick backward and forward,
along the notches, keeping time. The women
sung; and the sweetness of their voices exceeded
whatever I had heard before.

This entertainment lasted upward of an hour ;
and when it was finished a dance commenced.
The men formed themselves into a row on one
side, and the women on the other ; and each moved sidewise, first up, and then down the room.
The sound of bells and other jingling materials,
attached to the women's dresses, enabled them to

keep time. The songs and dances were continued alternately, till near midnight, when all our visitors departed.

These amusements were given to us complimentarily, by the chief. He took no part in the performances himself; but, sat smoking while they proceeded.

III. It had been my wish to go further on the Plains, till I should have reached the mountains, at the feet of which, as I have already observed, they lie; but, the chief informed me, that the latter were still at the distance of many days' journey, and that the intervening country was a tract destitute of the least appearance of wood. In the winter, as he asserted, this tract cannot be crossed at all; and in the summer, the traveller is in great danger of perishing for want of water; and the only fuel to be met with is the dung of the wild ox. It is intersected by a large river, which runs to the sun's rising, and which has its sources in the mountains.

With regard to the country of the Osinipoilles, he said, that it lay between the head of the Pasquayah, or Sascatchiwaine, and the country of the Sioux, or Nadowessies, who inhabit the heads of the Missisipi. On the west, near the mountains,

38

were the Snake Indians and Black-feet, troublesome neighbours, by whose hands numbers of his
warriors fell.

The Osinipoilles have many villages, composed
of from one to two hundred tents each. Few exceed
the latter number.   They often go to the mountains, on war-parties, and always on horseback.
When the great chief intends to go to war, he
sends messengers to the several villages, directing
the warriors to meet him at an appointed place and
time.   With regard to the latter, it is described
by the moon, as the beginning, full, or end.   In
obedience to the summons, they assemble in greater numbers than can be counted,* armed with the
bow, sling and spear, and with quivers full of arrows.—They have still another weapon, formed of
a stone of about two pounds weight, which is sewed in leather, and made fast to a wooden handle, two
feet long. In using it, the stone is whirled round the
handle, by a warrior sitting on horseback, and attack-
ing at full speed. Every stroke, which takes effect,
brings down a man, or horse; or, if used in the chase,
an ox. To prevent the weapon from slipping out of
the hand, a string, which is tied to the handle, is
also passed round the wrist of the wearer.   The
horses of the Osinipoilles were originally procured
from white people, with beards, who live to the

* This was the chief's expression.

southward ; that is, the Spanish colonists, in New-Mexico.

The animals, which I saw alive on the Plains, are oxen, red-deer and wolves ; but, I saw also the skins of foxes, bears, and a small number of panthers, sometimes called tigers, and most properly, *cougars*.*

IV. In their religious notions, as well as in their dress, arms and other particulars, there is a general agreement between the Osinipoilles and the Cristinaux.† They believe in a creator and governor of the world, in a future life, and in the spirits, gods, or *manitos*, whom they denominate *wakons*. Their practices of devotion consist in the singing of songs, accompanied by the drum, or rattle, or both ; and the subjects of which are prayers and praises : in smoking-feasts, or feasts of the pipe, or calumet, held in honour of the spirits, to whom the smoke of tobacco is supposed to be a most acceptable incense ; and in other feasts, as well as in fasts and in sacrifices. The victims of sacrifice are

---

* Felis concolor.

† Such of the Cristinaux as inhabit the Plains, have also their horses, like the Osinipoilles. By language, the Osinipoilles are allied to the Nadowessies ; but, they are always at war with them. Of the language of the Nadowessies, Carver has given a short vocabulary.

usually dogs, which being killed, and hung upon poles, are left there to decay.

V. Many travellers have described the marriages of the Indians; but, as they have greatly disagreed in their delineations, I shall venture to set down such particulars as have presented themselves to my immediate view. Though inserted here, they have no exclusive relation to the Osinipoilles; all the Indians, whom I have seen, having similar customs on this head.

A young man, desirous of marrying a particular young woman, visits the lodge in which she lives, at night, and when all the family, or rather families, are sleeping on their mats around. He comes provided with a match, or splint of wood, which he lights among the embers of one of the fires which are in the middle of the lodge. The only intention of this, is the very obvious one, of finding, by the help of the light, the young woman whom he means to visit, and whom, perhaps, he has to awaken. This done, he extinguishes the light. In speaking to her, he whispers, because it is not necessary to disturb all the lodge; and because something like privacy and secrecy belong to the nature of the occasion. If she makes no reply to his address, he considers his attempts at acquaintance as repulsed, and in consequence retires. If the young woman receives him with favour, he takes part of

her mat.   He brings with him his own blanket.——
I consider this practice as precisely similar to
the *bundling* of New-England, and other countries ; and, to say the least, as not more licentious.
Children, born out of wedlock, are very rare among
the Indians.

The lover, who is permitted to remain, retires
before day-break. When the young woman has consented to be his wife, he opens the affair to his own
mother, by whom it is communicated to her's ; and
if the two mothers agree, they mutually apply to
their husbands.

The father of the young man then invites the
father of the young woman to a stew, or sudatory,
prepared for the occasion, and at which he com-
municates the wishes of his son. The father of
the young woman gives no reply till the day following, when, in his own turn, he invites the other
to the sweating-house. If he approves of the match,
the terms upon which it is to be made are now
settled.

Stews, sudatories, or sweating-houses, are resorted to for cure of sickness, for pleasure, or for
giving freedom and vigour to the faculties of the
mind, when particular deliberation and sagacity are
called for. To prepare them for a guest, is, therefore, to offer every assistance to his judgment, and

manifest the reverse of a disposition to take an unfair advantage of him : it is the exact opposite of offering him liquor. They are constructed of slender branches of trees, united at the top, and closely covered with skins or blankets. Within, water is poured upon a red-hot stone, till the steam induces perspiration.

The terms are either, that the young man, as was most usual in older times, shall serve the father of the young woman for a certain period, (as for three years,) or that he shall redeem himself from this obligation by a present.

If he be to serve, then, at the time fixed, he goes, accompanied by his father and mother, to the lodge of the young woman's family. There, he is desired, by her mother, to sit down on the same mat with her. A feast is usually served, and the young woman's father delivers a suitable speech. The young man is thenceforward regarded as one of his wife's family, and remains in the lodge accordingly.

If, on the other hand, he redeems himself by a present, then his father and mother go alone to the lodge of the young woman's family, carrying a present. If the present be accepted, they leave it, and return home ; and, shortly after, the father and mother, accompanied by their daughter, go to the lodge of the bridegroom's family, where the bride is desired to sit down beside her husband. The feast and speech are now made by the young man's father, and the young woman is received into his family.

Every man marries as many wives as he pleases, and as he can maintain; and the usual number is from one to five. The oldest, in most cases, is the mistress of the family, and of the other wives among the rest. They appear to live in much harmony. Polygamy, among the Indians, conduces little to population. For the number of adults, the children are always few.

VI. In naming a child, the father officiates, and the ceremony is simple. The relations are invited to a feast, when he makes a speech, informing the guests of the name by which the child is to be called, and addresses a prayer to the Great Spirit, petitioning for the child's life and welfare.

VII. With respect to the burial of the dead, if the death happen in the winter-season, and at a distance from the burial-ground of the family, the body invariably accompanies all the wanderings and journeys of the survivors, till the spring, and till their arrival at the place of interment. In the mean time, it is every-where rested on a scaffold, out of the reach of beasts of prey. The grave is made of a circular form, about five feet deep, and lined with bark of the birch, or some other tree, or with skins. A seat is prepared, and the body is placed in a sitting posture, with supporters on either side. If the deceased be a man, his weapons of war, and of the chase, are buried with him, as also his shoes, and every thing for which, as a living warrior or hunter, he would have occasion, and, indeed, all his property ; and I believe that those, whose piety alone may not be strong enough to ensure to the dead the entire inventory of what is supposed to be necessary for them, or is their own, are compelled to do them justice by another argument, and which is, the fear of their displeasure. A defrauded or neglected ghost, although invisible, can disperse the game of the plains or forests, so that the hunter shall hunt in vain ; and, either in the chase or in the war, turn aside the arrow, or palsy the arm that draws the bow : in the lodge, it can throw a child into the fire.

The body and its accompaniments are covered with bark ; the bark with logs ; and the logs with earth. This done, a relation stands up, and pronounces an eulogium on the deceased, extolling his virtues, and relating his exploits. He dwells upon the enemies whom he slew, the scalps and prisoners which he took, his skill and industry in the chase, and his deportment as a father, husband, son, brother, friend, and member of the community. At each assertion which he makes, the speaker strikes a post, which is placed near the grave ; a gesture of asseveration, and which enforces the attention of the audience, and assists in counting up the points delivered. The eulogium finished, the post is painted,* and on it are represented the number of prisoners taken, by so many figures of men ; and of killed and scalped, by figures without heads. To these are added his badge, called, in the Algon-quin tongue, a *totem*, and which is in the nature of an armorial bearing. It informs the passing In-dian of the family to which the deceased belonged. A serious duty at the grave, is that of placing food, for the use of the dead, on the journey to the *land of souls*. This care is never neglected, even under every disadvantage of molestation. In the neighbourhood of the traders, dishes of cooked ve-nison are very commonly placed on the graves of those long buried, and as commonly removed by Europeans, even without offence to those who placed them there. In situations of great want, I have more than once resorted to them for food.

VIII. The men, among the Osinipoilles, are well made ; but, their colour is much deeper than that of the more northern Indians. Some of

---

* Hence, *The Painted Post*, the name of a village in Pennsylvania.

the women are tolerably handsome, considering
how they live, exposed to the extremes of heat
and cold, and placed in an atmosphere of smoke,
for at least one half of the year. Their dress
is of the same materials, and of the same form,
with that of the female Cristinaux. The married women suffer their hair to grow at random,
and even hang over their eyes. All the sex is
fond of garnishing the lower edge of the dress with
small bells, deer-hoofs, pieces of metal, or any
thing capable of making a noise. When they
move, the sounds keep time, and make a fantastic
harmony.

IX. The Osinipoilles treat with great cruelty
their slaves. As an example, one of the principal
chiefs, whose tent was near that which we occupied,
had a female slave, of about twenty years of age.
I saw her always on the outside of the door of the
tent, exposed to the severest cold ; and having
asked the reason, I was told, that *she was a slave.*
The information induced me to speak to her
master, in the hope of procuring some mitigation
of the hardships she underwent ; but, he gave me
for answer, that he had taken her on the other side
of the western mountains ; that at the same time he
had lost a brother and a son, in battle ; and that the
enterprise had taken place, in order to release one
of his own nation, who had been a slave in her's,

and who had been used with much greater severity
than that which she experienced.—The reality, of
the last of these facts, appeared to me to be impossible. The wretched woman fed and slept with
the dogs, scrambling with them for the bones
which were thrown out of the tent. When her
master was within, she was never permitted to enter ; at all seasons, the children amused themselves with impunity in tormenting her, thrusting
lighted sticks into her face ; and if she succeeded
in warding off these outrages, she was violently
beaten. I was not successful in procuring any
diminution of her sufferings ; but, I drew some
relief from the idea, that their duration could not
be long. They were too heavy to be sustained.

It is known, that some slaves have the good for-
tune to be adopted into Indian families, and are afterward allowed to marry in them; but, among the
Osinipoilles, this seldom happens ; and, even among
the Chipeways, where a female slave is so adopted
and married, I never knew her to lose the degrading
appellation of *wa'kan'*, *a slave.**

* This word, *wakan*, which, in the Algonquin language,
signifies *a slave*, is not to be confounded with *wakan*, or
wakon, which, in the language of the Nadowessies and
Osinipoilles, signifies a spirit, or *manito*.

CHAPTER XIV.

ON the nineteenth of February, the chief apprised us, that it was his design to depart the next morning for the fort. In consequence, we collected our baggage, which, however, was but small; consisting in a buffalo-robe for each person, an axe and a kettle. The last was reluctantly parted with by our friends, who had none left to supply its place.

At day-break, on the twentieth, all was noise and confusion in the camp; the women beating and loading the dogs, and the dogs howling and crying. The tents were speedily struck, and the coverings and poles packed up, to be drawn by the dogs.

Soon after sunrise, the march began. In the van were twenty-five soldiers, who were to beat the path, so that the dogs might walk. They were followed by about twenty men, apparently in rea- diness for contingent services ; and after these went the women, each driving one or two, and some, five loaded dogs. The number of these ani- mals, actually drawing loads, exceeded five hun- dred. After the baggage, marched the main body of the men, carrying only their arms. The rear was guarded by about forty soldiers. The line of march certainly exceeded three miles in length.

The morning was clear and calm. Our road was a different one from that by which we had reached the camp. We passed several herds of wild oxen, which betrayed some alarm at the noise of the dogs and women, resounding on every side.

Our march was pursued till sunset, when we reached a small wood, the first that we had seen all day. The great chief desired Mr. Patterson and myself to lodge in his own tent, and we accord- ingly became part of his family. We saw that his

entire and numerous household was composed of
relations.   The chief, after smoking his pipe, determined the line of march for the next day ; and
his dispositions in this regard were immediately
published through the camp.

At day-break, our tents were again struck, and
we proceeded on our march, in the same order as
the day before. To-day, (to follow the phraseology
of the Plains,) we had once *land in sight*, consisting
in two small *islands*, lying at a great distance from
our road.   On our march, the chief informed us,
that he proposed reaching another camp of his people that evening, and would take it with him to the
fort.   Accordingly, at about four o'clock in the afternoon, we discovered a wood, and presently afterward saw smoke rising from it.   At sunset, we
encamped near the wood, where we found a hundred tents.   We were not long arrived, before the
chiefs of this second camp paid a visit to the Great
Road, who informed them of his intention to visit
the fort, and recommended to them to join his
march.   They consented, and orders were given as
usual, by a public officer.

The night afforded me but little sleep, so great was
the disturbance, from noises of all kinds ;—feasting
and dancing ; the women chastising the dogs ; the
dogs of the two camps meeting, and maintaining

against each other, the whole night long, a universal war.

In the morning, the two camps united in one line
of march, which was now so far extended, that those
in the rear could not descry the front.　At noon,
we passed a small wood, where we saw horses feeding.　The Indians informed me, that they belonged to one of their camps, or villages; and that it
was their uniform custom to leave their horses,
in the beginning of winter, at the first wood where
they were when the snow fell, at which the
horses always remain through the season, and
where their masters are sure to find them in the
spring.　The horses never go out of sight of the
island assigned them, winter or summer, for fear
of wanting its shelter in a storm.

We encamped this evening among some small
brush-wood.　Our fire went out accidentally in the
night; and I was kept awake by the cold, and by
the noise of the dogs.

In the course of the next day, the twenty-third
of the month, we passed several coppices, and saw
that the face of the country was changing, and that
we had arrived on the margin of the Plains.　On
the twenty-seventh, we encamped on a large wood,
where the Indians resolved on leaving the old women and children, till their return from the fort,

from which we were now distant only one day's
march.   On the twenty-eighth, they halted for
the whole day ; but, we engaged two of them to
lead us forward, and thus arrived in the evening at
the fort, where we found all well.   A large band
of Cristinaux had brought skins from the Beaver
River.

Next day, the Indians advanced their camp to
within half a mile of the fort, but left thirty tents
behind them in the wood.   They continued with
us three days, selling their skins and provisions,
for trinkets.

It is not in this manner that the Northern Indians
dispose of the harvest of the chase. With them, the
principal purchases are of necessaries ; but, the
Osinipoilles are less dependent on our merchandise.
The wild ox alone supplies them with every thing
which they are accustomed to want.   The hide of
this animal, when dressed, furnishes soft clothing
for the women ; and, dressed with the hair on, it
clothes the men.   The flesh feeds them ; the si-
news afford them bow-strings ; and even the
paunch, as we have seen, provides them with that
important utensil, the kettle.   The amazing numbers of these animals prevent all fear of want ; a
fear which is incessantly present to the Indians of
the north.

On the fourth morning, the Osinipoilles departed. The Great Road expressed himself much satisfied with his reception, and he was well deserving of a good one ; for in no situation could strangers have been treated more hospitably than we were treated in his camp. The best of every thing it contained was given us.

The Osinipoilles, at this period, had had no acquaintance with any foreign nation, sufficient to affect their ancient and pristine habits. Like the other Indians, they were cruel to their enemies; but, as far as the experience of myself and other Europeans authorises me to speak, they were a harmless people, with a large share of simplicity of manners, and plain-dealing. They lived in fear of the Cristinaux, by whom they were not only frequently imposed upon, but pillaged, when the latter met their bands, in smaller numbers than their own.

As to the Cristinaux, they are a shrewd race of men, and can cheat, lie, and sometimes steal ; yet even the Cristinaux are not so much addicted to stealing as is reported of the Indians of the South Sea: their stealing is pilfering ; and they seldom pilfer any thing but *rum*, a commodity which tempts them beyond the power of resistance.

I remained at Fort des Prairies till the twenty-second of March, on which day I commenced my return to Beaver Lake.

Fort des Prairies, as already intimated, is built on the margin of the Pasquayah, or Sascatchiwaine, which river is here two hundred yards across, and flows at the depth of thirty feet below the level of its banks. The fort has an area of about an acre, which is enclosed by a good stockade, though formed only of poplar, or aspen-wood,* such as the country affords.   It has two gates, which are carefully shut every evening, and has usually from fifty to eighty men for its defence.

Four different interests were struggling for the Indian trade of the Sascatchiwaine ; but, fortunate-ly, they had this year agreed to join their stock, and when the season was over, to divide the skins and meat.   This arrangement was beneficial to the merchants ; but, not directly so to the Indians, who, having no other place to resort to, nearer than Hudson's Bay, or Cumberland House, paid greater prices than if a competition had subsisted.   A competition, on the other hand, afflicts the Indians with a variety of evils, in a different form.

---

* This fort, or one which occupied a contiguous site, was formerly known by the name of Fort aux Trembles.

The following were the prices of goods at Fort des Prairies :

A gun, - - -	20	beaver-skins.
A stroud blanket, -	10	do.
A white do. - -	8	do.
An axe, of one pound weight,	3	do.
Half a pint of gunpowder,	1	do.
Ten balls, - - -	1	do.

but, the principal profits accrued from the sale of knives, beads, flints, steels, awls and other small articles.

Tobacco, when sold, fetched one beaver-skin per foot of *Spencer's twist ;* and rum, not very strong, two beaver-skins per bottle : but, a great proportion of these commodities was disposed of in presents.

The quantity of furs brought into the fort was very great. From twenty to thirty Indians arrived daily, laden with packs of beaver-skins.

CHAPTER XV.

Author arrives at Beaver Lake. Subsistence be-
comes scarce. Supply of Water-fowl. Voyage
to the Missinipi. Voyage on the Missinipi, to-
ward Lake Arabuthcow, or Athabasca. Chepewy-
ans—Dress—Manners—authority of the Chiefs,
and their care of the People. Impositions of En-
glish Traders, and credulity of the Indians.
Voyage from the Missinipi to the Grand Portage.
Wild scene on Beaver Lake. Author, in company
with Mr. Frobisher, arrives at the Grand Por-
tage—and at Montréal.

THE days being now lengthened, and the snow
capable of bearing the foot, we travelled swiftly ;
and the weather, though cold, was very fine.

On the fifth of April, we arrived, without accident, at Cumberland House. On our way, we
saw nothing living, except wolves, who followed
us in great numbers, and against whom we were
obliged to use the precaution of maintaining large
fires at our encampments.

On the seventh, we left Cumberland House; and on the ninth, in the morning, reached our fort on Beaver Lake, where I had the pleasure of finding my friends well.

In my absence, the men had supported themselves by fishing; and they were all in health, with the exception of one, who was hurt at the Grand Portage, by a canoe's falling upon him.

On the twelfth, Mr. Thomas Frobisher, with six men, was despatched to the river Churchill, where he was to prepare a fort, and inform such Indians, as he might see on their way to Hudson's Bay, of the approaching arrival of his partners.

The ice was still in the same state as in January; but, as the season advanced, the quantity of fish diminished, insomuch that Mr. Joseph Frobisher and myself were obliged to fish incessantly; and often, notwithstanding every exertion, the men went supperless to bed. In a situation like this, the Canadians are the best men in the world; they rarely murmur at their lot, and their obedience is yielded cheerfully.

We continued fishing till the fifth of May, when we saw swans, flying toward the Maligne. From this circumstance, and from our knowledge of the rapidity of the current of that river, we supposed it was free from ice. In consequence, I proceeded thither, and arriving in the course of a day's journey, found it covered with swans, geese and other water-fowl, with which I soon loaded my sledge, and then returned to the fort.

The passage, toward the Churchill, being thus far open, we left our fort on the twenty-first of May, forty in number, and with no greater stock of provision than a single supper. At our place of encampment, we set our nets, and caught more fish than we had need of; and the same food was plenty with us all the way. The fish were pickerel and white-fish.

On the twenty-second, we crossed two carrying-places, of half a mile each, through a level country, with marshes on the border of the river. The sun now appeared above the horizon, at half past eight o'clock in the morning; and there was twilight all the time that he was below it. The men had but few hours for rest; for, after encamping, a supper was not only to be cooked, but caught, and it was therefore late before they went to sleep. Mr. Frobisher and myself rose at three; and the men were stirring still earlier, in order to take up the nets, so that we might eat our breakfast, and be on our journey, before sunrise.

On the sixth of June, we arrived at a large lake, which, to our disappointment, was entirely frozen over, and at the same time the ice was too weak to be walked upon. We were now fearful of detention for several days; but had the consolation to find our situation well supplied with fish. On the following night there was a fall of snow, which lay on the ground to the depth of a foot. The wind was from the north-east. The Indians who were of our party hunted, and killed several elks, or moose-deer. At length, the wind changed into the southern quarter, on which we had rain, and the snow melted. On the tenth, with some difficulty, we crossed the lake, which is twenty miles in length, through a channel opened in the ice. On the fifteenth, after passing several carrying-places, we reached the river Churchill, Missinibi, or Missinipi, where we found Mr. Thomas Frobisher and his men, who were in good health, and had built a house for our reception.

The whole country, from Beaver Lake to the Missinipi, is low near the water, with mountains in the distance. The uplands have a growth of small pine-trees, and the valleys, of birch and spruce. The river is called the *Churchill River*, from Fort Churchill, in Hudson's Bay, the most northerly of the company's factories or trading-houses, and which is seated at its mouth. By Mr. Joseph Frobisher, it was named *English River*. At the spot where our house was built, the river is five miles wide, and very deep. We were estimated, by the Indians, to be distant three hundredmiles from the sea. Cumberland House was to the southward of us, distant four hundred miles. We had the light of the sun, in sufficient quantity for all purposes, during the whole twenty-four hours. The redness of his rays reached far above the horizon.

We were in expectation of a particular band of Indians, and as few others made their appearance, we resolved on ascending the river to meet them, and even, in failure of that event, to go as far westward as Lake Arabuthcow,* distant, according to the Indians, four hundred and fifty miles.

With these views, we embarked on the sixteenth, with six Canadians, and also one Indian woman, in the capacity of a guide, in which service Mr. Frobisher had previously employed her.

As we advanced, we found the river frequently widening into lakes, thirty miles long, and so broad, as well as so crowded with islands, that we were unable to distinguish the main land on either side. Above them, we found a strait, in which the channel was shallow, rocky and broken, with the attendant features of *rapids* and carrying-places.

* Called also *Athapuscow*, and *Athabasca*.

The country was mountainous, and thinly wooded; and the banks of the river were continued rocks. Higher up, lofty mountains discovered themselves, destitute even of moss ; and it was only at intervals, that we saw afar off a few stunted pine-trees.

On the fifth day, we reached the Rapide du Serpent, which is supposed to be three hundred miles from our point of departure. We found white-fish so numerous, in all the rapids, that shoals of many thousands were visible, with their backs above the water. The men supplied themselves by killing them with their paddles. The water is clear and transparent.

The Rapide du Serpent, is about three miles long, and very swift. Above this, we reached another rapid, over the carrying-place of which we carried our canoe. At this place, vegetation began to re-appear; and the country became level, and of an agreeable aspect. Nothing human had hitherto discovered itself ; but, we had seen several bears, and two *cariboux*, on the sides of the mountains, without being able to kill any thing.

The course of the river was here from south to north. We continued our voyage till the twenty-fourth, when, a large opening being before us, we saw a number of canoes, filled with Indians, on

41

their voyage down the stream. We soon met each other, in the most friendly manner.

We made presents of tobacco to the chiefs, and were by them requested to put to shore, that we might encamp together, and improve our acquaintance. In a short time, we were visited by the chiefs, who brought us beaver-skins, in return for which we gave a second present ; and we now proposed to them to return with them to our fort, where we were provided with large quantities of such goods as they wanted. They received our proposal with satisfaction.

On the twenty-fifth of June, we embarked, with all the Indians in our company, and continued our voyage day and night, stopping only to boil our kettle. We reached our house on the first of July.

The Indians comprised two bands, or parties, each bearing the name of its chief, of whom one was called the Marten, and the other, the Rapid. They had joined for mutual defence, against the Cristinaux, of whom they were in continual dread. They were not at war with that nation, but subject to be pillaged by its bands.

While the lodges of the Indians were setting up, the chiefs paid us a visit, at which they received a large present of merchandise, and agreed to our request, that we should be permitted to purchase the furs of their bands.

They inquired, whether or not we had any rum ; and, being answered in the affirmative, they observed, that several of their young men had never tasted that liquor, and that if it was too strong it would affect their heads. Our rum was in consequence submitted to their judgment ; and, after tasting it several times, they pronounced it to be too strong, and requested that we would *order a part of the spirit to evaporate*. We complied, by adding more water, to what had received a large proportion of that element before ; and, this being done, the chiefs signified their approbation.

We remarked, that no other Indian approached our house, while the chiefs were in it. The chiefs observed to us, that their young men, while sober, would not be guilty of any irregularity ; but, that lest, when in liquor, they should be troublesome, they had ordered a certain number not to drink at all, but maintain a constant guard. We found their orders punctually obeyed ; and not a man attempted to enter our house, during all the night. I say, all the night ; because it was in the course of this night, the next day, and the night following, that our traffic was pursued and finished. The Indians delivered their skins at a small window, made for that purpose, asking, at the same time, for the different things they wished to purchase, and of which the prices had been previously settled with the chiefs. Of these, some were higher than those quoted from Fort des Prairies.

On the third morning, this little fair was closed ; and, on making up our packs, we found, that we had purchased twelve thousand beaver-skins, besides large numbers of otter and marten.

Our customers were from Lake Arabuthcow, of which, and the surrounding country, they were the proprietors, and at which they had wintered. They informed us, that there was, at the further end of that lake, a river, called Peace River, which descended from the Stony or Rocky Mountains, and from which mountains the distance to the *salt lake*, meaning the Pacific Ocean, was not great ; that the lake emptied itself by a river, which ran to the northward, which they called *Kiratchinini Sibi*,* or Slave River,† and which flows into another lake, called by the same name ; but, whether this lake was or was not the sea, or whether it emptied itself or not into the sea, they were unable to say. They were at war with the Indians who live

* Or *Y-atch-inini Sipi.*

† These are the rivers which have since been explored by Sir Alexander Mackenzie.

at the bottom of the river, where the water is salt.
They also made war on the people beyond the
mountains, toward the Pacific Ocean, to which
their warriors had frequently been near enough to
see it. Though we conversed with these people
in the Cree, or Cristinaux language, which is the
usual medium of communication, they were Chepewyans, or Rocky Mountain Indians.

They were in possession of several ultramon-
tane prisoners, two of whom we purchased : one,
a woman of twenty-five years of age; and the other,
a boy of twelve. They had both been recently taken, and were unable to speak the language of their
masters. They conversed with each other in a
language exceedingly agreeable to the ear, composed of short words, and spoken with a quick utter-
ance. We gave for each a gun.

The dress of the Chepewyans nearly resembled
that of the Cristinaux ; except that it was composed of beaver and marten-skins, instead of those of
the ox and elk. We found these people orderly
and unoffending ; and they appeared to consider
the whites as creatures of a superior order, to
whom every thing is known.

The women were dirty, and very inattentive to
their whole persons, the head excepted, which they
painted with red ochre, in defect of vermilion. Both

themselves, and their husbands for them, were forward in seeking a loose intercourse with the Europeans. The former appeared vain of solicitation, and having first obtained the consent of their husbands, afterward communicated to them their success. The men, who no doubt thought with the Cristinaux on this subject,* were the first to speak in behalf of their wives ; and were even in the practice of carrying them to Hudson's Bay, a journey of many hundred miles, on no other errand.

Having been fortunate enough to administer medical relief to one of these Indians, during their stay, I came to be considered as a physician, and found that this was a character held in high veneration. Their solicitude and credulity, as to drugs and nostrums, had exposed them to gross deceptions, on the part of the agents of the Hudson's Bay Company. One of the chiefs informed me, that he had been at the Bay the year before, and there purchased a quantity of medicines, which he would allow me to inspect. Accordingly, he brought a bag, containing numerous small papers, in which I found lumps of white sugar, grains of coffee, pepper, allspice, cloves, tea, nutmegs, ginger and other things of this kind, sold as specifics against evil spirits, and against the dangers of battle ; as giving power over enemies, and particularly the white bear, of which the Indians in these latitudes are much afraid :—others were infallible

* See page 249.

against barrenness in women ; against difficult la-
bours; and against a variety of other afflictions. In
a second parcel, I found small prints ; the identical
ones, which, in England, are commonly sold in
sheets to children, but each of which was here
transformed into a talisman, for the cure of some
evil, or obtention of some delight :—No. 1. "A
" sailor kissing his mistress, on his return from
" sea ;"—this, worn about the person of a gallant,
attracted, though concealed, the affections of the
sex ! No. 2. " A soldier in arms ;"—this poured
a sentiment of valour into the possessor, and gave
him the strength of a giant !

By means of these commodities, many customers were secured to the company ; and even
those Indians, who shortened their voyage by dealing with us, sent forward one canoe, laden with
beaver-skins, to purchase articles of this kind, at
Cumberland House.   I did not venture to dispute
their value.

This part of our commercial adventure completed, Mr. Frobisher and myself left the remainder
of our merchandise in the care of Mr. Thomas
Frobisher, who was to proceed with them to Lake
Arabuthcow ; and, on the fourth of July, set out on
our return to the Grand Portage.

In recrossing Beaver Lake, the wind obliged us
to put into a bay which I had not visited before.
Taking my gun, I went into the woods, in search
of game ; but, I had not advanced more than half a
mile, when I found the country almost inaccessi-
ble, by reason of masses of rock, which were scattered in all directions : some were as large as houses,
and lay as if they had been first thrown into the
air, and then suffered to fall into their present posture. By a circuitous route, I at last ascended the
mountain, from one side of which they had fallen ;
the whole body was fractured, and separated by large
chasms. In some places, parts of the mountain, of
half an acre in surface, were raised above the general level. It was a scene for the warfare of the
Titans, or for that of Milton's angels!

The river, which, when we first arrived at Cumberland House, had run with a swift current into
the Sascatchiwaine, now ran in a contrary direction, toward the lake. This was owing to the rise
of water in the Sascatchiwaine, from which same
cause all the lowlands were at this time overflowed.

Our twilight nights continued till we were to the
southward of Lake Winipegon. The weather was
so favourable, that we crossed that lake in six days;
though, in going, it took us thirty.

On an island in the Lake of the Woods, we saw several Indians, toward whom we made, in hopes to purchase provisions, of which we were much in want ; and whom we found full of a story, that some strange nation had entered Montréal, taken Québec, killed all the English, and would certainly be at the Grand Portage before we arrived there.

On my remarking to Mr. Frobisher, that I suspected the *Bastonnais* (Bostonians, or English colonists) had been doing some mischief in Canada, the Indians directly exclaimed, " Yes; " that is the name ! *Bastonnais*."—They were lately from the Grand Portage, and appeared seriously apprehensive that the *Bastonnais* were coming into the north-west.*

At the Forks of the River à la Pluie, there were a large number of Indians, under a friendly chief, with which latter I had had a previous acquaintance. On my visiting him, he told me, that there was bad news ; and then repeated the story which we had heard on the Lake of the Woods, adding, that some of his young men were evil inclined, and

---

*Bastonnais (*Bostonnais*, Bostonians) is the name by which the Canadians describe all the inhabitants of the English colonies, now the United States ; and in the north-west, the English traders commonly use the French language.

that he wished us immediately to depart. We were not deaf to the admonition, of the grounds of which we staid long enough to be convinced. We were roughly importuned for rum ; and one of the Indians, after we had embarked, fetched his gun, and fired at us twice, but without effect.

No further accident attended our voyage to the Grand Portage, from which place we pursued the route to Montréal, where we arrived on the fifteenth of October. We found the province delivered from the irruption of the colonists, and protected by the forces of General Burgoyne.

THE END.

I. RILEY, Printer.

ERRATA.

Page 36, note, for " Amicawac," read *Amicwac.*
66, line 7, for " south," read *Sault.*